DUINO ELEGIES
and THE SONNETS TO ORPHEUS

Christmas 2010

Corey, I hope you like this. Love Brian & Julie

Rainer Maria Rilke

DUINO ELEGIES
and THE SONNETS
TO ORPHEUS

Translated by A. Poulin, Jr.

Foreword by Mark Doty

A Mariner Book / Houghton Mifflin Company

Boston / New York

First Mariner Books edition 2005

For information about permission to reproduce selections from
this book, write to Permissions, Houghton Mifflin Company,
215 Park Avenue South, New York, New York 10003.

Visit our Web site: www.houghtonmifflinbooks.com.

The German text for this book is taken from Rilke's
Saemtliche Werke, Volume 1, copyright © 1955 by Insel
Verlag, Frankfurt am Main. All rights reserved.

Library of Congress Cataloging-in-Publication Data
Rilke, Rainer Maria, 1875–1926.
Duino Elegies and The Sonnets to Orpheus.
Translation of Duineser Elegien and Die Sonnette
an Orpheus.
English and German.
Includes bibliographical references.
ISBN 0-395-25015-3
ISBN 0-395-25058-7 (pbk.)
ISBN 0-618-56589-2 (pbk.)
ISBN 978-0-618-56589-4 (pbk.)
I. Rilke, Rainer Maria, 1875–1926. Die Sonnette an Orpheus.
English & German. 1977. II. Title: Duino Elegies.
PT2635.I65D82 1977
831'.9'12 76-47553

Printed in the United States of America

DOC 10 9 8 7 6 5

An earlier version of A. Poulin, Jr.'s translation of *Duino Elegies* was orig-
inally published as "A Special *APR* Supplement" by *The American Poetry
Review.* Some of *The Sonnets to Orpheus* originally appeared in *The Ameri-
can Poetry Review* and in *The Ohio Review.* Grateful acknowledgment is
made to the editors of these journals.

CONTENTS

FOREWORD TO THE MARINER EDITION

YEARS AGO, at Goddard College, a squirrelly little progressive school in Vermont committed to delighting and tormenting its students and faculty in equal measure, I taught a course in Rilke's work that was as much a writing workshop as a literature seminar. We began by reading every translation of "Archaic Torso of Apollo" I could find, in order to think about the relativity of translation. Many competing versions made the poem seem less a monumental, unapproachable thing than something made entirely of language, subject to reinvention and the ongoing work of interpretation. ("Archaic Torso of Apollo" *is* monumental, but it doesn't help readers, especially new ones, to think of it as such. A "masterpiece" can be an uninviting, sealed-off thing, like the poor *Mona Lisa*, not only shielded behind her acrylic barrier, but walled behind her nearly impassable reputation.)

From there we went on to *The Notebook of Malte Laurids Brigge*, and the students' first assignment was to write, as Rilke had in the opening sections of that weird and gripping book, about the experience of being a stranger. From then on, they were hooked; they were caught in Rilke's project, twinned to it, as it were, writing with him. We moved through many poems, and ended with the *Duino Elegies*, read aloud and talked through, sentence by sentence. I'm not sure I ever had a richer adventure as a teacher. There is a way that meaning resides in poems themselves, but surely the most beautiful of meanings is that made by readers, together, discovering the complexities before them, opening a poem for one another. It is intrinsically pleasurable to talk about great poems in a group; it enlarges the life of reading, and brings the poem into the moment's community in a profound way.

On the final day of class, we arrived at the last of the Elegies. It was the beginning of December, and someone suggested we go out into the garden. Taking turns, passage by passage, we read the Tenth Elegy aloud, in the first sparse falling snow of the season. It sounds a little silly now to say what we did, but there was nothing false or pretentious about the experience as we lived it. We were a group of people who'd come to be bound together in the voice of a poet dead sixty years; his poems had been giving all of us, whatever our age or situation, instruction in how to live. To stand in the sudden enlivening shift of weather, in a ruined garden, around an empty fountain—that felt exactly right. Snowflakes on the pages of our open books. A little snow on our tongues, and phrases both bracing and a bit frightening at once, consoling and startling. That's the character of what makes us feel more alive: it exhilarates and saddens, enlivens and unsettles. *Every angel's terrifying.* The worldly, exterior garden was a broken thing, but the interior fountain was abundant.

My experience in Vermont was one of many readings of Rilke's great poem, and of its attendant lyrical distillation and outcry, *The Sonnets to Orpheus.* Like all great poems, they simply seem to rewrite themselves before you as you read. Their capacity to delight and to provoke does not weary with time; the Rilke one reads as a teenager is not the one that speaks to us at thirty, or looms at forty-five. Thus my young students read a book about the problem of finding purpose in living, and about the difficulties of love. I read that poem, too, but the pressing questions of evanescence darkened the text for me like a dye. It wasn't that my students didn't see that coloring, but rather that it couldn't be, for them, the primary element. My course was in 1988 or 1989, and the Rilke I read was speaking to me about the terrifying pressures of the AIDS epidemic, midway through fifteen years of crisis in American life.

It is not a distortion of a great poem to read it in this way. In fact, it's what the poet longs for: that the poem be taken to heart, addressing the need and the hour. That whatever the poet's personal stake—the particular stuff of a life—has been somehow embodied and then relinquished, so that the reader can inhabit the poem. This seems the rarest sort of artistic selflessness, and it is accomplished, paradoxically, only through an act of inscribing the self on the page with such conviction, such exacting dedication, and such interest in the someday reader's experience that what is merely of the biographical self can be burned away in poetry's annealing fire. What is on the page, ultimately, is no longer the subject but a version of the subjectivity. That is why poems like these have a startling sense of freshness about them, like new snow; subjectivity is held there in suspension, and it does not age.

Thus it matters not a bit, really, the famous romance of Rilke's composition of these poems: their opening voice arriving on a cliffside wind beside a borrowed castle, the first rush of composition, and then the long wait through a war and years of silence that might well never have ended. And then the solitary tower, the ferocious outrush of the poem, and the gift of the sonnet sequence immediately thereafter—all just months before the poet's death, begun by pricking his thumb on a rose. What a lovely and unlikely story. It's a tale an American poet of our era can only dimly countenance; it posits a degree of artistic isolation and of privilege hard for us to think we might share. The closest I've ever come to it was at an artists' colony in Italy, high on a ridge that splits Lake Como in two, in a villa that actually belonged once to the Princess von Thurn und Taxis-Hohenlohe, to whom the Elegies are dedicated. Perhaps Rilke himself visited there. I used to walk through the villa garden to my studio, a little stone tower, and throw open the wooden shutters over my desk to the unglazed window's astonishing rectangle of Alps. It's a dream of the poet's life that engenders among us as much suspicion as longing.

And that leads to the virtue of Poulin's translation, this direct and straightforward version that has not been out of print since the day it was published. That must be because it has continued to matter to readers, to connect (*O Orpheus sings! O tall tree in the ear!*)

My first attempt to read these poems foundered on the grand but relatively inaccessible language of J. B. Leishman and Stephen Spender. What was a young writer schooled in a midcentury plainsong—raised on the flattened declarative syntax of Bly and Simic, Wright and Strand—to make of the archaic glories of the Rilke translations we had?

I loved that unavailable music, but I could not *use* it, not in the way I could bring the stuff of the great Rilkean moments into my own life in these new renderings:

> And these things, whose lives
> are lived in leaving—they understand when you praise them.
> Perishing, they turn to us, the most perishable, for help.
> They want us to change them completely in our invisible hearts,
> oh—forever—into us! Whoever we may finally be.
> Earth, isn't this what you want: to resurrect
> in us invisibly? Isn't it your dream
> to be invisible one day? Earth! Invisible!
> What's your urgent charge, if not transformation?
> Earth, my love, I will.

That last sentence was the one that mattered to me most, at twenty-two, when I read these translations first; it was a promise, a compact one might make with experience. It spoke to the possibility of an insight far beyond me, and of the embodiment of that understanding in a grand linguistic structure.

At thirty-five, reading with my students, this was a book of anticipatory and actual grief, a handbook of the spirit in the face of impermanence. Now, at fifty-one, what strikes me most is the glory of Rilke's faith in the transformative, preserving word. In language as the signature of vision, the container made to survive us. In the collective project of rendering reality into speech. (That seems even braver, finally, in the face of the world war that preceded the composition of these poems, than Rilke's nerve, in the last of the Elegies, to simply walk past death, on toward the Next.)

These are great modernist texts of dissatisfaction, or perhaps it would be more accurate to say great texts of modern dissatisfaction, and the search for a means to live, here where *the wind / full of outer space gnaws at our faces.* The Elegies are the intellectual evocation of this problem; they release tremendous emotional energy through an act of inquiry. The sonnets are a wild welling up of song, in which feeling comes first—but, because they are great poems, that feeling leads inescapably to the energies of the intellect, through which the poems build a monument not simply to the lost girl to whom they are dedicated, but to all that disappears.

And to the act of speaking, of singing itself. Rilke has the almost unimaginable authority to proclaim that as our purpose, the rescue of mortal earth into less mortal word. This is an extremely hard-won act of making faith, and a nearly impersonal sort of consolation, which is probably the only kind of consolation the experience of the twentieth century will allow us to believe.

It is also the most literary of credos imaginable: that the work of "saying the world" is a kind of participatory redemption. These poems are both the testament of that faith and its demonstration.

Mark Doty
January 2005

PERSONAL ACKNOWLEDGMENTS

I WANT TO THANK The National Endowment for the Arts and The Research Foundation of the State University of New York for grants I received while working on these translations, as well as the P.E.N. American Center for assistance in time of need. I also want to thank Kirsten Michalski, Galen Williams, Inés Delgado de Torres, and Leonard Randolph personally for kindness that far exceeded professional courtesy.

Grateful acknowledgment is due to Mr. Kurt Bernheim, Insel Verlag's representative in the United States, for his gracious assistance in securing the reprint and translations rights to Rilke's poems for this book.

Irma Pylyshenko and Christoph Kaiser, my colleagues at the State University of New York at Brockport, generously agreed to read various parts and stages of my manuscript for the sake of accuracy, as did Professor Jack Stein (Harvard University), Stephen Conway (Boston University), and Paul Hopper (Pennsylvania State University). Their expertise and sensitivity elucidated difficult passages and afforded me insights that were invaluable in my attempt to make these translations as faithful to the original as I believed possible.

My friend Stephen Berg initially suggested that I translate the *Duino Elegies*. From my first faltering attempts to the version that appeared in *The American Poetry Review*, he offered me advice and encouragement with editiorial acumen and with that fine sensibility that marks his own poems and translations. Bertrand Mathieu, Rimbaud's brilliant translator, gave me the kind of help and encouragement that can come only from a long-time friend, poet, scholar, and blood brother — all of which he is.

Jonathan Galassi suggested that I translate *The Sonnets to Or-*

pheus in order that this book include both of Rilke's last major sequences. His professional vigor as my editor was surpassed only by his friendship, his sustained loyalty, and by the personal interest he devoted to these translations.

And you, Love, for wintering out a hard-turned year.

A. P., Jr.

PREFACE

IN HIS NOTED LETTER of 1925 to Witold von Hulewicz, his Polish translator, Rilke stated that the *Duino Elegies* and *Sonnets to Orpheus* "are, as could not be otherwise, of the same 'birth' " and "filled with the same essence." Since he wrote all of the Sonnets and completed most of the Elegies in an astoundingly short period of time (almost entirely within the month of February, 1922*), Rilke's claim that these two sequences of poems "support each other constantly" is entirely plausible. Moreover, critics and scholars generally agree that an attentive reading of the Elegies and Sonnets reveals that they do support and reaffirm each other and are clearly filled with the same essential sensibility, artistry, and vision that distinguishes them as Rilke's greatest achievement and one of the most fully realized artistic statements of twentieth-century poetry.

This book marks the first time that English translations of these two major works are being published together as the larger interdependent whole they've always been. I've attempted to make the Elegies and Sonnets as fully accessible as translations can be to individuals who can't read German, to remain as faithful as possible to the original, and to make them successful poems in English. Since these are a poet's work and not a scholar's, readers of German will note that my attempt to be faithful to the original can't be equated with an intention to

---

* Rilke started writing the Elegies in 1912 and worked on them intermittently until 1914. For a number of reasons, he did not and could not return to them again until 1922. According to several of his letters, between February 2 and 5 of 1922 he wrote the first sequence of sonnets; by February 9 he had completed 7 elegies; on February 11 he had completed 10 elegies; and by February 20, not only had he written still another elegy (now the Fifth) but also the second sequence of sonnets.

be literal. I've taken such liberties as I felt were necessitated by the differences between the two languages and by Rilke's unique logic and imagery, as well as by his occasional idiosyncratic use of German. At times I've taken even greater liberties because a more literal translation didn't seem to convey the full aesthetic sense of given passages. On such occasions I invoked Rilke's own articulation of the poet's (and the translator's) responsibility and risk: "And he obeys, even as he oversteps the bounds."

In his letters, Rilke spoke of the Elegies and especially of the Sonnets as "dictations" that were "entrusted" to him. Such words may no longer be part of the idiom of contemporary poetry; nevertheless, the translator is entrusted with a kind of dictation, and one of the poet-translator's responsibilities is to try to submerge his personal sensibility into that of the poet whose work he is translating. But he can't annihilate his own inner poetic sense entirely. The translation that results from such an encounter thus becomes a fusion of languages, cultures, historical moments, and aesthetic personalities; it becomes a third poem.

No less important to this kind of alchemical process and its results is the fact that, when dealing with poems like the Elegies and Sonnets, one can't ignore the work of others or avoid indebtedness. Like so many others of my generation, I was introduced to these poems through J. B. Leishman and Stephen Spender's translation of the *Duino Elegies* and M. D. Herter Norton's versions of *The Sonnets to Orpheus*. Later I read C. F. MacIntyre's translations of the Elegies and Sonnets and, more recently, Stephen Garmey and Jay Wilson's Elegies, as well as David Young's courageous rendition of them. Such distinguished contemporary American poets as Randall Jarrell, Robert Bly, and W. D. Snodgrass have also published translations of some of the Sonnets. I've read all of them, I've learned from all of them, and now and then I've stolen a word, a phrase, a line from one or more of them. It's simply foolhardy to try to improve on what is obviously a *mot juste*. I hope someone else will find a word or phrase to steal from these versions.

When the work at hand is as monumental and awesome as the *Duino Elegies* and *Sonnets to Orpheus*, Emerson's dictum that each age must write its own books takes on a new meaning. Each age, each generation needs many versions of great works in translation in order to know them as variously and acutely as possible, and to come to a fuller realization that there have been a few among us, like Rilke, who haven't failed to use our "generous spaces" and who still assert: "That's us . . . This stood among men."

A. Poulin, Jr.
Brockport, New York
February, 1976

DUINO ELEGIES

DUINESER ELEGIEN

Aus dem Besitz der Fürstin
Marie von Thurn und Taxis-Hohenlohe

DUINO ELEGIES

The Property of
Princess Marie von Thurn und Taxis-Hohenlohe

DIE ERSTE ELEGIE

Wer, wenn ich schriee, hörte mich denn aus der *Engel*
Ordnungen? und gesetzt selbst, es nähme
einer mich plötzlich ans Herz: ich verginge von seinem
stärkeren Dasein. Denn das Schöne ist nichts
[5] als des Schrecklichen Anfang, den wir noch grade extragen,
und wir bewundern es so, weil es gelassen verschmäht,
uns zu zerstören. Ein jeder Engel ist schrecklich.
Und so verhalt ich mich denn und verschlucke den
                      Lockruf
dunkelen Schluchzens. Ach, wen vermögen
[10] wir denn zu brauchen? Engel nicht, Menschen nicht,
und die findigen Tiere merken es schon,
daß wir nicht sehr verläßlich zu Haus sind
in der gedeuteten Welt. Es bleibt uns vielleicht
irgend ein Baum an dem Abhang, daß wir ihn täglich
[15] wiedersähen; es bleibt uns die Straße von gestern
und das verzogene Treusein einer Gewohnheit,
der es bei uns gefiel, und so blieb sie und ging nicht.
O und die Nacht, die Nacht, wenn der Wind voller
                      Weltraum
uns am Angesicht zehrt —, wem bliebe sie nicht, die ersehnte,
[20] sanft enttäuschende, welche dem einzelnen Herzen
mühsam bevorsteht. Ist sie den Liebenden leichter?
Ach, sie verdecken sich nur mit einander ihr Los.
Weißt du's *noch* nicht? Wirf aus den Armen die Leere
zu den Räumen hinzu, die wir atmen; vielleicht daß die
                      Vögel

THE FIRST ELEGY

And if I cried, who'd listen to me in those angelic
orders? Even if one of them suddenly held me
to his heart, I'd vanish in his overwhelming
presence. Because beauty's nothing
but the start of terror we can hardly bear,   [5]
and we adore it because of the serene scorn
it could kill us with. Every angel's terrifying.
  So I control myself and choke back the lure
of my dark cry. Ah, who can we turn to,
then? Neither angels nor men,   [10]
and the animals already know by instinct
we're not comfortably at home
in our translated world. Maybe what's left
for us is some tree on a hillside we can look at
day after day, one of yesterday's streets,   [15]
and the perverse affection of a habit
that liked us so much it never let go.
  And the night, oh the night when the wind
full of outer space gnaws at our faces; that wished for,
gentle, deceptive one waiting painfully for the lonely   [20]
heart — she'd stay on for anyone. Is she easier on lovers?
But they use each other to hide their fate.
  You *still* don't understand? Throw the emptiness in
your arms out into that space we breathe; maybe birds

[25] die erweiterte Luft fühlen mit innigerm Flug.

Ja, die Frühlinge brauchten dich wohl. Es muteten manche
Sterne dir zu, daß du sie spürtest. Es hob
sich eine Woge heran im Vergangenen, oder
da du vorüberkamst am geöffneten Fenster,
[30] gab eine Geige sich hin. Das alles war Auftrag.
Aber bewältigtest du's? Warst du nicht immer
noch von Erwartung zerstreut, als kündigte alles
eine Geliebte dir an? (Wo willst du sie bergen,
da doch die großen fremden Gedanken bei dir
[35] aus und ein gehn und öfters bleiben bei Nacht.)
Sehnt es dich aber, so singe die Liebenden; lange
noch nicht unsterblich genug ist ihr berühmtes Gefühl.
Jene, du neidest sie fast, Verlassenen, die du
so viel liebender fandst als die Gestillten. Beginn
[40] immer von neuem die nie zu erreichende Preisung;
denk: es erhält sich der Held, selbst der Untergang war
                                 ihm
nur ein Vorwand, zu sein: seine letzte Geburt.
Aber die Liebenden nimmt die erschöpfte Natur
in sich zurück, als wären nicht zweimal die Kräfte,
[45] dieses zu leisten. Hast du der Gaspara Stampa
denn genügend gedacht, daß irgend ein Mädchen,
dem der Geliebte entging, am gesteigerten Beispiel
dieser Liebenden fühlt: daß ich würde wie sie?
Sollen nicht endlich uns diese ältesten Schmerzen
[50] fruchtbarer werden? Ist es nicht Zeit, daß wir liebend
uns vom Geliebten befrein und es bebend bestehn:
wie der Pfeil die Sehne besteht, um gesammelt im
                                 Absprung

will feel the air thinning as they fly deeper into themselves.   [25]

Yes, Springs needed you. Many stars
waited for you to see them. A wave
that had broken long ago swelled toward you,
or when you walked by an open window, a violin
gave itself. All that was your charge.   [30]
But could you live up to it? Weren't you always
distracted by hope, as if all this promised
you a lover? (Where would you have hidden her,
with all those strange and heavy thoughts
flowing in and out of you, often staying overnight?)   [35]
When longing overcomes you, sing about great lovers;
their famous passions still aren't immortal enough.
You found that the deserted, those you almost envied,
could love you so much more than those you loved.
Begin again. Try out your impotent praise again;   [40]
think about the hero who lives on: even his fall
was only an excuse for another life, a final birth.
But exhausted nature draws all lovers back
into herself, as if there weren't the energy
to create them twice. Have you remembered   [45]
Gaspara Stampa well enough? From that greater love's
example, any girl deserted by her lover
can believe: "If only I could be like her!"
Shouldn't our ancient suffering be more
fruitful by now? Isn't it time our loving freed   [50]
us from the one we love and we, trembling, endured:
as the arrow endures the string, and in that gathering
momentum

mehr zu sein als er selbst. Denn Bleiben ist nirgends.

Stimmen, Stimmen. Höre, mein Herz, wie sonst nur
[55] Heilige hörten: daß sie der riesige Ruf
aufhob vom Boden; sie aber knieten,
Unmögliche, weiter und achtetens nicht:
So waren sie hörend. Nicht, daß du *Gottes* ertrügest
[60] die Stimme, bei weitem. Aber das Wehende höre,
die ununterbrochene Nachricht, die aus Stille sich bildet.
Es rauscht jetzt von jenen jungen Toten zu dir.
Wo immer du eintratst, redete nicht in Kirchen
zu Rom und Neapel ruhig ihr Schicksal dich an?
Oder es trug eine Inschrift sich erhaben dir auf,
[65] wie neulich die Tafel in Santa Maria Formosa.
Was sie mir wollen? leise soll ich des Unrechts
Anschein abtun, der ihrer Geister
reine Bewegung manchmal ein wenig behindert.

Freilich ist es seltsam, die Erde nicht mehr zu bewohnen,
[70] kaum erlernte Gebräuche nicht mehr zu üben,
Rosen, und andern eigens versprechenden Dingen
nicht die Bedeutung menschlicher Zukunft zu geben;
das, was man war in unendlich ängstlichen Händen,
nicht mehr zu sein, und selbst den eigenen Namen
[75] wegzulassen wie ein zerbrochenes Spielzeug.
Seltsam, die Wünsche nicht weiterzuwünchen. Seltsam,
alles, was sich bezog, so lose im Raume
flattern zu sehen. Und das Totsein ist mühsam
und voller Nachholn, daß man allmählich ein wenig
[80] Ewigkeit spürt. — Aber Lebendige machen

becomes more than itself. Because to stay is to be nowhere.

Voices, voices. My heart, listen as only
saints have listened: until some colossal   [55]
sound lifted them right off the ground; yet,
they listened so intently that, impossible
creatures, they kept on kneeling. Not that you could
endure the voice of God! But listen to the breathing,
the endless news growing out of silence,   [60]
rustling toward you from those who died young.
Whenever you entered a church in Rome or Naples,
didn't their fate always softly speak to you?
Or an inscription raised itself to reach you,
like that tablet in Santa Maria Formosa recently.   [65]
What do they want from me? That I gently wipe away
the look of suffered injustice sometimes
hindering the pure motion of spirits a little.

It's true, it's strange not living on earth
anymore, not using customs you hardly learned,   [70]
not giving the meaning of a human future
to roses and other things that promise so much;
no longer being what you used to be
in hands that were always anxious,
throwing out even your own name like a broken toy.   [75]
It's strange not to wish your wishes anymore. Strange
to see the old relationships now loosely fluttering
in space. And it's hard being dead and straining
to make up for it until you can begin to feel
a trace of eternity. But the living are wrong   [80]

alle den Fehler, daß sie zu stark unterscheiden.
Engel (sagt man) wüßten oft nicht, ob sie unter
Lebenden gehn oder Toten. Die ewige Strömung
reißt durch beide Bereiche alle Alter
[85]   immer mit sich und übertönt sie in beiden.

Schließlich brauchen sie uns nicht mehr, die Früheentrückten,
man entwöhnt sich des Irdischen sanft, wie man den Brüsten
milde der Mutter entwächst. Aber wir, die so große
Geheimnisse brauchen, denen aus Trauer so oft
[90]   seliger Fortschritt entspring — : *könnten* wir sein ohne sie?
Ist die Sage umsonst, daß einst in der Klage um Linos
wagende erste Musik dürre Erstarrung durchdrang;
daß erst im erschrockenen Raum, dem ein beinah göttlicher
                                                    Jüngling
plötzlich für immer enttrat, das Leere in jene
[95]   Schwingung geriet, die uns jetzt hinreißt und tröstet und hilft.

*

to make distinctions that are too absolute.
Angels (they say) often can't tell whether
they move among the living or the dead.
The eternal torrent hurls all ages through
both realms forever and drowns out their voices in both.   [85]

At last, those who left too soon don't need us anymore;
we're weaned from the things of this earth as gently
as we outgrow our mother's breast. But we, who need
such great mysteries, whose source of blessed progress
so often is our sadness — could we exist without them?   [90]
Is the story meaningless, how once during the lament for
                                            Linos,
the first daring music pierced the barren numbness,
and in that stunned space, suddenly abandoned
by an almost godlike youth, the Void first felt
that vibration which charms and comforts and helps us   [95]
                        now?

*

DIE ZWEITE ELEGIE

Jeder Engel ist schrecklich. Und dennoch, weh mir,
ansing ich euch, fast tödliche Vögel der Seele,
wissend um euch. Wohin sind die Tage Tobiae,
da der Strahlendsten einer stand an der einfachen Haustür,
[5]   zur Reise ein wenig verkleidet und schon nicht mehr
                furchtbar;
(Jüngling dem Jüngling, wie er neugierig hinaussah).
Träte der Erzengel jetzt, der gefährliche, hinter den Sternen
eines Schrittes nur nieder und herwärts: hochauf-
schlagend erschlüg uns das eigene Herz. Wer seid ihr?

[10] Frühe Geglückte, ihr Verwöhnten der Schöpfung,
Höhenzüge, morgenrötliche Grate
aller Erschaffung, — Pollen der blühenden Gottheit,
Gelenke des Lichtes, Gänge, Treppen, Throne,
Räume aus Wesen, Schilde aus Wonne, Tumulte
[15] stürmisch entzückten Gefühls und plötzlich, einzeln,
Spiegel: die die entströmte eigene Schönheit
wiederschöpfen zurück in das eigene Antlitz.

Denn wir, wo wir fühlen, verflüchtigen; ach wir
atmen uns aus und dahin; von Holzglut zu Holzglut
[20] geben wir schwächern Geruch. Da sagt uns wohl einer:
ja, du gehst mir ins Blut, dieses Zimmer, der Frühling
füllt sich mit dir . . . Was hilfts, er kann uns nicht halten,
wir schwinden in ihm und um ihn. Und jene, die schön sind,
o wer hält sie zurück? Unaufhörlich steht Anschein

THE SECOND ELEGY

Every angel's terrifying. Almost deadly birds
of my soul, I know what you are, but, oh,
I still sing to you! What happened to the days of Tobias
when one of you stood in a simple doorway, partly
disguised for the trip, radiant, no longer appalling;   [5]
(a young man to the young man as he looked out amazed).
If the archangel, the dangerous one behind the stars,
took just one step down toward us today: the quicker
pounding of our heart would kill us. Who are you?

Fortunate first ones, creation's pampered darlings,   [10]
ranges, mountain tops, morning-red ridges
of all Beginning — seed of a blossoming god,
hinges of light, hallways, stairways, thrones,
spaces of being, force fields of ecstasy, storms
of unchecked rapture, and suddenly, separate,   [15]
mirrors: each drawing its own widespread
streaming beauty back into its face.

But we: we vanish in our feelings. Oh, we breathe
ourselves out, and out; our smell dissolves
from ember to ember. It's true, someone may tell us: [20]
"You're in my blood, this room, Spring floods
with you . . ." What good is it? He can't hold us.
We vanish in him and around him. And the beautiful,
oh, who can hold them back? Some look is always rising

[25]   auf in ihrem Gesicht und geht fort. Wie Tau von dem Frühgras
hebt sich das Unsre von uns, wie die Hitze von einem
heißen Gericht. O Lächeln, wohin? O Aufschaun:
neue, warme, entgehende Welle des Herzens — ;
weh mir: wir *sinds* doch. Schmeckt denn der Weltraum,
[30]   in den wir uns lösen, nach uns? Fangen die Engel
wirklich nur Ihriges auf, ihnen Entströmtes,
oder ist manchmal, wie aus Versehen, ein wenig
unseres Wesens dabei? Sind wir in ihre
Züge soviel nur gemischt wie das Vage in die Gesichter
[35]   schwangerer Frauen? Sie merken es nicht in dem Wirbel
ihrer Rückkehr zu sich. (Wie sollten sie's merken.)

Liebende könnten, verstünden sie's, in der Nachtluft
wunderlich reden. Denn es scheint, daß uns alles
verheimlicht. Siehe, die Bäume *sind;* die Häuser,
[40]   die wir bewohnen, bestehn noch. Wir nur
ziehen allem vorbei wie ein luftiger Austausch.
Und alles ist einig, uns zu verschweigen, halb als
Schande vielleicht und halb als unsägliche Hoffnung.

Liebende, euch, ihr in einander Genügten,
[45]   frag ich nach uns. Ihr greift euch. Habt ihr Beweise?
Seht, mir geschiehts, daß meine Hände einander
inne werden oder daß mein gebrauchtes
Gesicht in ihnen sich schont. Das giebt mir ein wenig
Empfindung. Doch wer wagte darum schon zu *sein?*
[50]   Ihr aber, die ihr im Entzücken des anderen
zunehmt, bis er euch überwältigt
anfleht: nicht *mehr* — ; die ihr unter den Händen

in their faces, and falling. Like dew on new grass,   [25]
like heat from a steaming dish, everything we are rises
away from us. O smile, where are you going?
O upturned look: new, warm, the heart's receding wave —
it hurts me, but that's what we are. Does the cosmic
space we dissolve into taste of us, then? Do angels   [30]
really absorb only what poured out of them,
or sometimes, as if by mistake, is there a trace
of us, too? Do the contours of their features bear
as much of us as that vague look on a pregnant woman's
face? Unnoticed by them in their whirling back   [35]
into themselves. (Why should they notice.)

If they were understood, lovers might say marvelous
things in the night air. Because it seems everything
wants to camouflage us. Look, trees exist;
the houses we live in still hold up. But we   [40]
pass by all of it like an exchange of breath.
Everything conspires to ignore us, half out of shame,
perhaps, half out of some speechless hope.

 Lovers, satisfied with each other, I'm asking you
about us. You hold each other. What's your proof?   [45]
Look, sometimes it happens my hands become aware
of each other, or my worn out face seeks shelter
in them. Then I feel a slight sensation.
But who'd dare to exist just for that?
Yet you, who grow in the other's ecstasy   [50]
until he's overcome and begs: "No more!";
you, who in one another's hands grow

euch reichlicher werdet wie Traubenjahre;
die ihr manchmal vergeht, nur weil der andre
[55]   ganz überhand nimmt: euch frag ich nach uns. Ich weiß,
ihr berührt euch so selig, weil die Liebkosung verhält,
weil die Stelle nicht schwindet, die ihr, Zärtliche,
zudeckt; weil ihr darunter das reine
Dauern verspürt. So versprecht ihr euch Ewigkeit fast
[60]   von der Umarmung. Und doch, wenn ihr der ersten
Blicke Schrecken besteht und die Sehnsucht am Fenster,
und den ersten gemeinsamen Gang, *ein* Mal durch den Garten:
Liebende, *seid* ihrs dann noch? Wenn ihr einer dem andern
euch an den Mund hebt und ansetzt —: Getränk an Getränk:
[65]   o wie entgeht dann der Trinkende seltsam der Handlung.

Erstaunte euch nicht auf attischen Stelen die Vorsicht
menschlicher Geste? war nicht Liebe und Abschied
so leicht auf die Schultern gelegt, als wär es aus anderm
Stoffe gemacht als bei uns? Gedenkt euch der Hände,
[70]   wie sie drucklos beruhen, obwohl in den Torsen die Kraft steht.
Diese Beherrschten wußten damit: so weit sind wirs,
dieses ist unser, uns *so* zu berühren; stärker
stemmen die Götter uns an. Doch dies ist Sache der Götter.

Fänden auch wir ein reines, verhaltenes, schmales
[75]   Menschliches, einen unseren Streifen Fruchtlands
zwischen Strom und Gestein. Denn das eigene Herz
                                         übersteigt uns
noch immer wie jene. Und wir können ihm nicht mehr
nachschaun in Bilder, die es besänftigen, noch in
[79]   göttliche Körper, in denen es größer sich mäßigt.

*

more abundant like grapes in a vintage year;
you, who sometimes disappear, but only when the other
takes over completely, I'm asking you about us.   [55]
I know why you touch each other so ecstatically:
that touch *lasts*. That place you cover with such
tenderness doesn't vanish, because you feel a pure
duration there. In your embrace you almost find
the promise of eternity. And yet, when you've survived   [60]
the fear of that first look, the longing at the window,
and that first walk in the garden, once: lovers,
are you still the same? When you lift yourselves
up to each other's lips and begin, drink for drink —
oh how strangely the drinker then slips from the role.   [65]

Didn't the caution of human gestures on Attic steles
amaze you? Weren't love and separation placed
on those shoulders so lightly they seemed made
of other stuff than we are? Remember the hands:
despite the power in the torso, they lie weightless.   [70]
The self-controlled knew this: we can only go this far.
All we can do is touch one another like this. The gods
can press down harder on us, but that's the gods' affair.

If only we could find something pure, contained,
narrow, human — our own small strip of orchard   [75]
between river and rock. For our heart rises
out of us as it did out of the others. And we can't
follow it any longer into figures that tame it, or
into godlike bodies where it finds a greater mastery.   [79]

*

DIE DRITTE ELEGIE

Eines ist, die Geliebte zu singen. Ein anderes, wehe,
jenen verborgenen schuldigen Fluß-Gott des Bluts.
Den sie von weitem erkennt, ihren Jüngling, was weiß er
selbst von dem Herren der Lust, der aus dem Einsamen oft,
[5]   ehe das Mädchen noch linderte, oft auch als wäre sie nicht,
ach, von welchem Unkenntlichen triefend, das Gotthaupt
aufhob, aufrufend die Nacht zu unendlichem Aufruhr.
O des Blutes Neptun, o sein furchtbarer Dreizack.
O der dunkele Wind seiner Brust aus gewundener Muschel.
[10] Horch, wie die Nacht sich muldet und höhlt. Ihr Sterne,
stammt nicht von euch des Liebenden Lust zu dem Antlitz
seiner Geliebten? Hat er die innige Einsicht
in ihr reines Gesicht nicht aus dem reinen Gestirn?

Du nicht hast ihm, wehe, nicht seine Mutter
[15] hat ihm die Bogen der Braun so zur Erwartung gespannt.
Nicht an dir, ihn fühlendes Mädchen, an dir nicht
bog seine Lippe sich zum fruchtbarern Ausdruck.
Meinst du wirklich, ihn hätte dein leichter Auftritt
also erschüttert, du, die wandelt wie Frühwind?
[20] Zwar du erschrakst ihm das Herz; doch ältere Schrecken
stürzten in ihn bei dem berührenden Anstoß.
Ruf ihn . . . du rufst ihn nicht ganz aus dunkelem Umgang.
Freilich, er *will*, er entspringt; erleichtert gewöhnt er
sich in dein heimliches Herz und nimmt und beginntsich.
[25] Aber begann er sich je?
Mutter , *du* machtest ihn klein, du warsts, die ihn anfing;

THE THIRD ELEGY

To sing about someone you love is one thing; but, oh,
the blood's hidden guilty river-god is something else.
Known to her only from a distance, what can her lover,
even, say about the lord of passion, who often out of
loneliness, before she could comfort him, often as if   [5]
she didn't exist, raised his godhead, oh, who knows from
what depths, came streaming, and incited the night to riot.
Oh that Neptune of the blood and his terrible trident!
Oh the dark wind of his chest from that twisted conch!
Listen, how the night carves itself out and grows hollow.   [10]
You stars, doesn't a lover's longing for his loved one's
face come from you? Doesn't his most intimate insight
into her purest face come from your own purest constellation?

No, it really wasn't you, nor was it his mother
who arched his brow with so much expectation.   [15]
Girl who's holding him now, not for yours,
not for your lips did his thicken with passion.
You who wander like the morning breeze, do you really
think your gentle coming could convulse him so?
True, you scared his heart; but more ancient terrors   [20]
rushed into him with your shocking touch. Call him . . .
you can't quite call him back from that dark circle.
Yes, he tries, he does escape; relieved, he starts
to feel at home in your comfortable heart and takes
and begins himself. But did he ever begin himself?   [25]
Mother, you made him small, you started him once;

dir war er neu, du beugtest über die neuen
Augen die freundliche Welt und wehrtest der fremden.
Wo, ach, hin sind die Jahre, da du ihm einfach
[30]   mit der schlanken Gestalt wallendes Chaos vertratst?
Vieles verbargst du ihm so; das nächtlich-verdächtige Zimmer
machtest du harmlos, aus deinem Herzen voll Zuflucht
mischtest du menschlichern Raum seinem Nacht-Raum
                                                hinzu.
Nicht in die Finsternis, nein, in dein näheres Dasein
[35]   hast du das Nachtlicht gestellt, und es schien wie aus
                                                Freundschaft.
Nirgends ein Knistern, das du nicht lächelnd erklärtest,
so als wüßtest du längst, *wann* sich die Diele benimmt . . .
Und er horchte und linderte sich. So vieles vermochte
zärtlich dein Aufstehn; hinter den Schrank trat
[40]   hoch im Mantel sein Schicksal, und in die Falten des
                                                Vorhangs
paßte, die leicht sich verschob, seine unruhige Zukunft.

Und er selbst, wie er lag, der Erleichterte, unter
schläfernden Lidern deiner leichten Gestaltung
Süße lösend in den gekosteten Vorschlaf — :
[45]   *schien* ein Gehüteter . . . Aber *innen*: wer wehrte,
hinderte innen in ihm die Fluten der Herkunft?
Ach, da *war* keine Vorsicht im Schlafenden; schlafend,
aber träumend, aber in Fiebern: wie er sich ein-ließ.
Er, der Neue, Scheuende, wie er verstrickt war,
[50]   mit des innern Geschehns weiterschlagenden Ranken
schon zu Mustern verschlungen, zu würgendem Wachstum,
                                                zu tierhaft

he was new to you; over those new eyes you arched
the friendly world and shut the strange one out.
Oh, where are the years when you simply stood between
him and the surging chaos with your slender body?   [30]
You hid so much from him then; at night you made
the threatening room harmless, your heart's sanctuary
mingling a more human space with his own night-space.
No, you didn't put the night-light in that darkness
but in your own nearer presence, and it glowed, friendly.   [35]
There wasn't a creak you couldn't explain with a smile,
as if you'd always known just when the floor would do that . . .
And he listened and was comforted. Coming to him quietly,
you could do so much; his tall, cloaked destiny stepped
behind the wardrobe, and his restless future that got out   [40]
of hand so easily molded itself to the curtains' folds.

    And lying there, relieved, mingling the sweetness
of your slight body with the first taste
of approaching sleep under his heavy lids,
he seemed protected . . . But inside: who could   [45]
stop or turn the floods of Origin in him?
Oh, there was no caution in that sleeper; sleeping,
but feverish and dreaming: what he dared!
So young and shy, how he entangled himself
in the spreading roots of events inside him,   [50]
twisted patterns, strangling tendrils, shapes

jagenden Formen. Wie er sich hingab —. Liebte.
Liebte sein Inneres, seines Inneren Wildnis,
diesen Urwald in ihm, auf dessen stummem Gestürztsein

[55] lichtgrün sein Herz stand. Liebte. Verließ es, ging die
eigenen Wurzeln hinaus in gewaltigen Ursprung,
wo seine kleine Geburt schon überlebt war. Liebend
stieg er hinab in das ältere Blut, in die Schluchten,
wo das Furchtbare lag, noch satt von den Vätern. Und jedes

[60] Schreckliche kannte ihn, blinzelte, war wie verständigt.
Ja, das Entsetzliche lächelte . . . Selten
hast du so zärtlich gelächelt, Mutter. Wie sollte
er es nicht lieben, da es ihm lächelte. *Vor* dir
hat ers geliebt, denn, da du ihn trugst schon,

[65] war es im Wasser gelöst, das den Keimenden leicht macht.

Siehe, wir lieben nicht, wie die Blumen, aus einem
einzigen Jahr; uns steigt, wo wir lieben,
unvordenklicher Saft in die Arme. O Mädchen,
dies: daß wir liebten *in* uns, nicht Eines, ein Künftiges,
                                     sondern

[70] das zahllos Brauende; nicht ein einzelnes Kind,
sondern die Väter, die wie Trümmer Gebirgs
uns im Grunde beruhn; sondern das trockene Flußbett
einstiger Mütter — ; sondern die ganze
lautlose Landschaft unter dem wolkigen oder

[75] reinen Verhängnis — : *dies* kam dir, Mädchen, zuvor.

Und du selber, was weißt du — , du locktest
Vorzeit empor in dem Liebenden. Welche Gefühle
wühlten herauf aus entwandelten Wesen. Welche

of preying animals. How he surrendered. — Loved.
Loved his interior world, the jungle in him, that
primal inner forest where his pale green heart stood
among the fallen and mute ruins. Loved. Then left it,   [55]
going out from his own roots into violent Beginning
where his own tiny birth was already outlived. Loving,
he stepped down into the older blood, into the canyons
where terror lurked, still gorged with fathers.
And every horror knew him, winked, and seemed to
                                        understand.   [60]
Yes, the hideous smiled at him . . . O mother,
you hardly ever smiled at him so tenderly.
How could he help but love whatever smiled at him?
He'd loved it before you; even while you carried him, it was
already dissolved in the water that makes the seed light.   [65]

   Look, we don't love like flowers
with only one season behind us; when we love,
a sap older than memory rises in our arms. O girl,
it's like this: inside us we haven't loved just some one
in the future, but a fermenting tribe; not just one   [70]
child, but fathers, cradled inside us like ruins
of mountains, the dry riverbed
of former mothers, yes, and all that
soundless landscape under its clouded
or clear destiny — girl, all this came before you.   [75]

And you yourself, how could you know — you've stirred
up prehistoric time in your lover. What feelings
welled up from beings no longer here.

Frauen haßten dich da. Wasfür finstere Männer
[80]   regtest du auf im Geäder des Jünglings? Tote
Kinder wollten zu dir . . . O leise, leise,
tu ein liebes vor ihm, ein verläßliches Tagwerk, — führ ihn
nah an den Garten heran, gieb ihm der Nächte
Übergewicht . . .
[85]   Verhalt ihn . . .

*

What women hated you. What sinister men
you incited in his young veins. Dead children   [80]
reached for you . . . Gently, oh, gently
do a good day's work for him each day, with love,
lead him toward the garden, give him those compensating
nights . . .
        Hold him back . . .   [85]

*

DIE VIERTE ELEGIE

O Bäume Lebens, o wann winterlich?
Wir sind nicht einig. Sind nicht wie die Zug-
vögel verständigt. Überholt und spät,
so drängen wir uns plötzlich Winden auf
[5]   und fallen ein auf teilnahmslosen Teich.
Blühn und verdorrn ist uns zugleich bewußt.
Und irgendwo gehn Löwen noch und wissen,
solang sie herrlich sind, von keiner Ohnmacht.

Uns aber, wo wir Eines meinen, ganz,
[10]   ist schon des andern Aufwand fühlbar. Feindschaft
ist uns das Nächste. Treten Liebende
nicht immerfort an Ränder, eins im andern,
die sich versprachen Weite, Jagd und Heimat.
Da wird für eines Augenblickes Zeichnung
[15]   ein Grund von Gegenteil bereitet, mühsam,
daß wir sie sähen; denn man ist sehr deutlich
mit uns. Wir kennen den Kontur
des Fühlens nicht: nur, was ihn formt von außen.
Wer saß nicht bang vor seines Herzens Vorhang?
[20]   Der schlug sich auf: die Szenerie war Abschied.
Leicht zu verstehen. Der bekannte Garten,
und schwankte leise: dann erst kam der Tänzer.
Nicht *der.* Genug! Und wenn er auch so leicht tut,
er ist verkleidet und er wird ein Bürger
[25]   und geht durch seine Küche in die Wohnung.
Ich will nicht diese halbgefüllten Masken,

THE FOURTH ELEGY

O trees of life, when is your winter?
Our nature's not the same. We don't have the instinct
of migrant birds. Late and out of season,
we suddenly throw ourselves to the wind
and fall into indifferent ponds. We   [5]
understand flowering and fading at once.
And somewhere lions still roam: so magnificent
they can't understand weakness.

Even when fully intent on one thing,
we feel another's costly tug. Hostility   [10]
is second nature to us. Having promised
one another distance, hunting, and home,
don't lovers always cross each other's boundaries?
    Then for the sketchwork of an eye-wink,
a contrasting background's painfully prepared   [15]
to make us see it. Because it's very clear
we don't know the contours of our feeling,
but only what shapes it from without.
    Who hasn't sat anxious in front of his heart's
curtain? It would go up: another parting scene.   [20]
Easy to understand. The familiar garden
swaying slightly; then came the dancer.
Not *him*. Enough! However graceful he may be,
he's disguised, turns into a suburbanite,
and walks into his house through the kitchen.   [25]
    I don't want these half-filled masks.

lieber die Puppe. Die ist voll. Ich will
den Balg aushalten und den Draht und ihr
Gesicht aus Aussehn. Hier. Ich bin davor.
[30]   Wenn auch die Lampen ausgehn, wenn mir auch
gesagt wird: Nichts mehr — , wenn auch von der Bühne
das Leere herkommt mit dem grauen Luftzug,
wenn auch von meinen stillen Vorfahrn keiner
mehr mit mir dasitzt, keine Frau, sogar
[35]   der Knabe nicht mehr mit dem braunen Schielaug:
Ich bleibe dennoch. Es giebt immer Zuschaun.

Hab ich nicht recht? Du, der um mich so bitter
das Leben schmeckte, meines kostend, Vater,
den ersten trüben Aufguß meines Müssens,
[40]   da ich heranwuchs, immer wieder kostend
und, mit dem Nachgeschmack so fremder Zukunft
beschäftigt, prüftest mein beschlagnes Aufschaun, —
der du, mein Vater, seit du tot bist, oft
in meiner Hoffnung, innen in mir, Angst hast,
[45]   und Gleichmut, wie ihn Tote haben, Reiche
von Gleichmut, aufgiebst für mein bißchen Schicksal,
hab ich nicht recht? Und ihr, hab ich nicht recht,
die ihr mich liebtet für den kleinen Anfang
Liebe zu euch, von dem ich immer abkam,
[50]   weil mir der Raum in eurem Angesicht,
da ich ihn liebte, überging in Weltraum,
in dem ihr nicht mehr wart . . . wenn mir zumut ist,
zu warten vor der Puppenbühne, nein,
so völlig hinzuschaun, daß, um mein Schauen
[55]   am Ende aufzuwiegen, dort als Spieler

I'd rather have a doll. That's whole.
I'll put up with the empty body, the wire, and
the face that's only surface. Here. I'm waiting.
Even if the lights go out; even if   [30]
I'm told, ''That's all''; even if emptiness
drifts toward me in gray drafts from the stage;
even if none of my silent ancestors
will sit next to me anymore, not a woman,
not even the boy with the squinting brown eyes —   [35]
I'll stay here. One can always watch.

Aren't I right? Father, you who found
life so bitter after tasting mine,
the first opaque infusion of my must,
as I kept growing, you kept on tasting   [40]
and, fascinated by the aftertaste
of such a strange future, tried my clouded gaze —
you, my father, who in my deepest hope
so often since your death have been afraid for me
and, serene, surrendered the kingdoms of serenity   [45]
the dead own, just for my bit of fate —
aren't I right? And aren't I right,
you who loved me for that first small impulse
of love for you I always turned from,
because the space in your faces, even while   [50]
I loved it, changed into outer space
where you no longer were . . . when I'm in the mood
to wait in front of the puppet stage — No,
to stare into it so intensely that finally
an angel must appear, an actor to counteract   [55]

ein Engel hinmuß, der die Bälge hochreißt.
Engel und Puppe: dann ist endlich Schauspiel.
Dann kommt zusammen, was wir immerfort
entzwein, indem wir da sind. Dann entsteht
[60]   aus unsern Jahreszeiten erst der Umkreis
des ganzen Wandelns. Über uns hinüber
spielt dann der Engel. Sieh, die Sterbenden,
sollten sie nicht vermuten, wie voll Vorwand
das alles ist, was wir hier leisten. Alles
[65]   ist nicht es selbst. O Stunden in der Kindheit,
da hinter den Figuren mehr als nur
Vergangnes war und vor uns nicht die Zukunft.
Wir wuchsen freilich und wir drängten manchmal,
bald groß zu werden, denen halb zulieb,
[70]   die andres nicht mehr hatten, als das Großsein.
Und waren doch, in unserem Alleingehn,
mit Dauerndem vergnügt und standen da
im Zwischenraume zwischen Welt und Spielzeug,
an einer Stelle, die seit Anbeginn
[75]   gegründet war für einen reinen Vorgang.

Wer zeigt ein Kind, so wie es steht? Wer stellt
es ins Gestirn und giebt das Maß des Abstands
ihm in die Hand? Wer macht den Kindertod
aus grauem Brot, das hart wird, — oder läßt
[80]   ihn drin im runden Mund, so wie den Gröps
von einem schönen Apfel? . . . Mörder sind
leicht einzusehen. Aber dies: den Tod,
den ganzen Tod, noch *vor* dem Leben so
sanft zu enthalten und nicht bös zu sein,
[85]   ist unbeschreiblich.

*

my stare and pull up the empty skins.
Angel and doll: a real play at last.
Then what we continually divide
by our being here unites there.
Then the cycle of all change can finally   [60]
rise out of our seasons. Then the angel
plays over and above us. Look at the dying,
surely they suspect how everything we do
is full of sham, here where nothing
is really itself. O hours of childhood,   [65]
when more than the mere past was behind
each shape and the future wasn't stretched out
before us. We were growing; sometimes we hurried
to grow up too soon, half for the sake of those
who had nothing more than being grown-up.   [70]
Yet when we were alone, we still amused
ourselves with the everlasting and stood there
in that gap between world and toy,
in a place which, from the very start,
had been established for a pure event.   [75]

Who'll show a child just as he is? Who'll set
him in his constellation and put the measure
of distance in his hand? Who'll make the death
of a child out of gray bread growing hard — or
leave it there in his round mouth like the core   [80]
of a sweet apple . . . ? Murderers are
easily understood. But this: to hold
death, the whole of death, so gently,
even before life's begun and not be mad
— that's beyond description!   [85]

*

DIE FÜNFTE ELEGIE
Frau Hertha Koenig zugeeignet

Wer aber *sind* sie, sag mir, die Fahrenden, diese ein wenig
Flüchtigern noch als wir selbst, die dringend von früh an
wringt ein *wem, wem* zu Liebe
niemals zufriedener Wille? Sondern er wringt sie,
[5]   biegt sie, schlingt sie und schwingt sie,
wirft sie und fängt sie zurück; wie aus geölter,
glatterer Luft kommen sie nieder
auf dem verzehrten, von ihrem ewigen
Aufsprung dünneren Teppich, diesem verlorenen
[10] Teppich im Weltall.
Aufgelegt wie ein Pflaster, als hätte der Vorstadt-
Himmel der Erde dort wehe getan.
                      Und kaum dort,
aufrecht, da und gezeigt: des Dastehns
[15] großer Anfangsbuchstab . . . , schon auch, die stärksten
Männer, rollt sie wieder, zum Scherz, der immer
kommende Griff, wie August der Starke bei Tisch
einen zinnenen Teller.

Ach und um diese
[20] Mitte, die Rose des Zuschauns:
blüht und entblättert. Um diesen
Stampfer, den Stempel, den von dem eignen
blühenden Staub getroffen, zur Scheinfrucht
wieder der Unlust befruchteten, ihrer
[25] niemals bewußten, — glänzend mit dünnster

THE FIFTH ELEGY
Dedicated to Frau Hertha von Koenig

But tell me, who are they, these troupers,
even more transient than us, obsessed since childhood,
and — for whose, whose sake? — wrung
by an insatiable will? But it wrings them,
bends them, swings and twists them,   [5]
tosses and catches them; and they fall,
as if through oiled and polished air,
on the threadbare carpet worn
thin by their endless leaping,
this carpet lost in space.   [10]
Stretched like a plaster, as if the suburban
sky had bruised the earth.
        And barely there,
erect, the essence of standing-there: the large initial
of Debut or Done — but even the strongest   [15]
men are tossed up again in play by that always
returning grip, like a pewter platter
Augustus the Strong once played with at his table.

And, oh, the rose of audience
blooms and sheds   [20]
around this center. Around
this pestle, this pistil pregnant with its own pollen,
fertilized again into the false fruit of
their own unconscious boredom, gleaming
with a synthetic smile, the flimsy   [25]

Oberfläche leicht scheinlächelnden Unlust.

Da: der welke, faltige Stemmer,
der alte, der nur noch trommelt,
eingegangen in seiner gewaltigen Haut, als hätte sie früher
[30] *zwei* Männer enthalten, und einer
läge nun schon auf dem Kirchhof, und er überlebte den
                        andern,
taub und manchmal ein wenig
wirr, in der verwitweten Haut.

Aber der junge, der Mann, als wär er der Sohn eines
                        Nackens
[35] und einer Nonne: prall und strammig erfüllt
mit Muskeln und Einfalt.

Oh ihr,
die ein Leid, das noch klein war,
einst als Spielzeug bekam, in einer seiner
[40] langen Genesungen . . .

Du, der mit dem Aufschlag,
wie nur Früchte ihn kennen, unreif,
täglich hundertmal abfällt vom Baum der gemeinsam
erbauten Bewegung (der, rascher als Wasser, in wenig
[45] Minuten Lenz, Sommer und Herbst hat) —
abfällt und anprallt ans Grab:
manchmal, in halber Pause, will dir ein liebes
Antlitz entstehn hinüber zu deiner selten
zärtlichen Mutter; doch an deinen Körper verliert sich,

patina of their boredom.

There the withered, wrinkled weightlifter,
old and merely drumming now, shriveled
up in his powerful skin that looks as if
it held two men once, and now one's   [30]
already lying in the churchyard, and he's
outlived the other, deaf and a little
weird in his widowed skin.

But the young one, the man, like the offspring
of a neck and nun: taut and tense,   [35]
filled with muscle and simplicity.

O you,
a still small pain
received as a plaything once
during one of its long convalescences . . .   [40]

You, who fall a hundred times
a day, with the thud only green fruit
know, out of that tree rising from
a cooperation of motion (rushing faster than water
through autumn, spring, and summer in minutes) —   [45]
you fall and bounce on the grave:
sometimes, half pausing, you feel a look
of love for your seldom tender mother
surge up to your face; then it loses itself

[50]   der es flächig verbraucht, das schüchtern
       kaum versuchte Gesicht . . . Und wieder
       klatscht der Mann in die Hand zu dem Ansprung, und eh
                       dir
       jemals ein Schmerz deutlicher wird in der Nähe des immer
       trabenden Herzens, kommt das Brennen der Fußsohln
[55]   ihm, seinem Ursprung, zuvor mit ein paar dir
       rasch in die Augen gejagten leiblichen Tränen.
       Und dennoch, blindlings,
       das Lächeln . . .

       Engel! o nimms, pflücks, das kleinblütige Heilkraut.
[60]   Schaff eine Vase, verwahrs! Stells unter jene, uns *noch*
                       nicht
       offenen Freuden; in lieblicher Urne
       rühms mit blumiger schwungiger Aufschrift:
                   »*Subrisio Saltat.*«.
         Du dann, Liebliche,
[65]   du, von den reizendsten Freuden
       stumm Übersprungne. Vielleicht sind
       deine Fransen glücklich für dich — ,
       oder über den jungen
       prallen Brüsten die grüne metallene Seide
[70]   fühlt sich unendlich verwöhnt und entbehrt nichts.
       Du,
       immerfort anders auf alle des Gleichgewichts schwankende
                       Waagen
       hingelegte Marktfrucht des Gleichmuts,
       öffentlich unter den Schultern.

[75]   Wo, o *wo* ist der Ort — ich trag ihn im Herzen — ,

in your body whose surface quickly absorbs that rippling,   [50]
shy, barely tried expression . . . And again
the man's hands are clapping for that leaping;
and before a pain has gotten near
your ever galloping heart, the burning
in the soles of your feet arrives ahead of   [55]
its own spring, chasing a few live
tears into your eyes. And yet,
your blind smile . . .

Angel, oh take it! Pluck that small-flowered healing herb!
Make a vase, preserve it! Set it among those joys   [60]
not open to us yet. In a lovely urn,
praise it with a high-flown, flowery inscription:

                              "Subrisio Saltat."

    Then you, darling,
you, silently leapt over   [65]
by the most exciting joys. Maybe
your hems are happy for you —
or over your firm young breasts
the green metallic silk
feels always indulged and lacking nothing.   [70]
You,
always on the swaying scales of balance
like stacked fruit of serenity
publicly displayed between shoulders.

Where, where is that place — I carry it in my heart —   [75]

wo sie noch lange nicht *konnten*, noch von einander
abfieln, wie sich bespringende, nicht recht
paarige Tiere; —
wo die Gewichte noch schwer sind;
[80]   wo noch von ihren vergeblich
wirbelnden Stäben die Teller
torkeln . . .

Und plötzlich in diesem mühsamen Nirgends, plötzlich
die unsägliche Stelle, wo sich das reine Zuwenig
[85]   unbegreiflich verwandelt —, umspringt
in jenes leere Zuviel.
Wo die vielstellige Rechnung
zahlenlos aufgeht.

Plätze, o Platz in Paris, unendlicher Schauplatz,
[90]   wo die Modistin, *Madame Lamort*,
die ruhlosen Wege der Erde, endlose Bänder,
schlingt und windet und neue aus ihnen
Schleifen erfindet, Rüschen, Blumen, Kokarden, künstliche
Früchte —, alle
unwahr gefärbt, — für die billigen
[95]   Winterhüte des Schicksals.
. . . .

Engel!: Es wäre ein Platz, den wir nicht wissen, und dorten,
auf unsäglichem Teppich, zeigten die Liebenden, die's hier
bis zum Können nie bringen, ihre kühnen
hohen Figuren des Herzschwungs,

where they still never could, where they still
fell apart like mating animals
poorly paired;
where weights are still heavy,
where their hoops still   [80]
totter away from their
futile twirling sticks . . . ?

And suddenly, in this tiresome nowhere, suddenly
in this indescribable place where the pure Too-Little
mysteriously changes — springs around   [85]
into an empty Too-Much.
Where the staggering bill
adds up to zero.

Squares, o square in Paris, endless showplace,
where the *modiste*, Madame Lamort,   [90]
twists and winds the restless ways of the world,
those endless ribbons, and from them designs
new bows, frills, flowers, cockades, artificial
fruit — all cheaply dyed — for the paltry
winter hats of fate.   [95]

. . . .

Angel: if there were a place we know nothing about,
and there, on some ineffable carpet, lovers revealed
everything that's impossible here: the daring
patterns of their high-flying hearts,

[100] ihre Türme aus Lust, ihre
       längst, wo Boden nie war, nur an einander
       lehnenden Leitern, bebend, — und *könntens*,
       vor den Zuschauern rings, unzähligen lautlosen Toten:
         Würfen die dann ihre letzten, immer ersparten,
[105] immer verborgenen, die wir nicht kennen, ewig
       gültigen Münzen des Glücks vor das endlich
       wahrhaft lächelnde Paar auf gestilltem
[108] Teppich?

*

their pyramids of passion, their ladders leaning   [100]
long, only on each other, where there was never
any ground, trembling — and if they could, in front
of those rings of spectators, the countless silent dead:
  Would they throw their last, always hoarded,
always hidden, unknown to us, forever valid   [105]
coins of happiness for that couple whose smile
was genuine at last, out there on that calmed
carpet?   [108]

*

DIE SECHSTE ELEGIE

Feigenbaum, seit wie lange schon ists mir bedeutend,
wie du die Blüte beinah ganz überschlägst
und hinein in die zeitig entschlossene Frucht,
ungerühmt, drängst dein reines Geheimnis.
[5]   Wie der Fontäne Rohr treibt dein gebognes Gezweig
abwärts den Saft und hinan: und er springt aus dem Schlaf,
fast nicht erwachend, ins Glück seiner süßesten Leistung.
Sieh: wie der Gott in den Schwan.
              . . . Wir aber verweilen,
[10]   ach, uns rühmt es zu blühn, und ins verspätete Innre
unserer endlichen Frucht gehn wir verraten hinein.
Wenigen steigt so stark der Andrang des Handelns,
daß sie schon anstehn und glühn in der Fülle des Herzens,
wenn die Verführung zum Blühn wie gelinderte Nachtluft
[15]   ihnen die Jugend des Munds, ihnen die Lider berührt:
Helden vielleicht und den frühe Hinüberbestimmten,
denen der gärtnernde Tod anders die Adern verbiegt.
Diese stürzen dahin: dem eigenen Lächeln
sind sie voran, wie das Rossegespann in den milden
[20]   muldigen Bildern von Karnak dem siegenden König.

Wunderlich nah ist der Held doch den jugendlich Toten.
                Dauern
ficht ihn nicht an. Sein Aufgang ist Dasein; beständig
nimmt er sich fort und tritt ins veränderte Sternbild
seiner steten Gefahr. Dort fanden ihn wenige. Aber,
[25]   das uns finster verschweigt, das plötzlich begeisterte
                Schicksal

THE SIXTH ELEGY

Fig tree, you've been so meaningful to me so long —
the way you almost completely neglect to bloom
and then, without fanfare, pour your purest
secret into the season's determined fruit.
Your arched branches drive the sap up and down   [5]
like a fountain's pipe; hardly awake, it leaps out of
sleep into the ecstasy of its sweetest accomplishment.
See, like the god into the swan . . .

                      But we linger;
oh, we glory in our flowering, and so we come to   [10]
the retarded core of our last fruit already betrayed.
In a few the surge of action rises so strongly that,
when the temptation to bloom touches the youth
of their mouths, of their eyelids, like gentle night air,
they're already standing and glowing with full hearts;   [15]
only in heroes, perhaps, and in those destined to die young,
those in whom death the gardener has twisted the veins
differently. They plunge ahead of their own laughter
like the team of horses in front of the lovingly
chiseled reliefs of the conquering King at Karnak.   [20]

The hero strangely resembles those who die young.
                    Survival
doesn't concern him. His rising is his Being. Time and
                       again
he takes off and charges into the changed constellation
of his constant danger. Only a few find him there. But
hiding the rest of us in darkness, suddenly infatuated,   [25]

singt ihn hinein in den Sturm seiner aufrauschenden Welt.
Hör ich doch keinen wie *ihn.* Auf einmal durchgeht mich
mit der strömenden Luft sein verdunkelter Ton.

Dann, wie verbärg ich mich gern vor der Sehnsucht:
                             O wär ich,
[30]   wär ich ein Knabe und dürft es noch werden und säße
in die künftigen Arme gestützt und läse von Simson,
wie seine Mutter erst nichts und dann alles gebar.

War er nicht Held schon in dir, o Mutter, begann nicht
dort schon, in dir, seine herrische Auswahl?
[35]   Tausende brauten im Schooß und wollten *er* sein,
aber sieh: er ergriff und ließ aus — , wählte und konnte.
Und wenn er Säulen zerstieß, so wars, da er ausbrach
aus der Welt deines Leibs in die engere Welt, wo er weiter
wählte und konnte. O Mütter der Helden, o Ursprung
[40]   reißender Ströme! Ihr Schluchten, in die sich
hoch von dem Herzrand, klagend,
schon die Mädchen gestürzt, künftig die Opfer dem
                            Sohn.
Denn hinstürmte der Held durch Aufenthalte der
                         Liebe,
jeder hob ihn hinaus, jeder ihn meinende Herzschlag,
[45]   abgewendet schon, stand er am Ende der Lächeln, —
                            anders.

*

fate sings him into the storm of its roaring world.
I don't hear anyone like him. All of a sudden, carried
by the streaming air, his dark song rushes through me.

Then how I'd like to hide from this longing. Oh I wish,
I wish it were still to come, and I was a boy sitting   [30]
propped up on my future arms, reading about Samson,
how at first his mother bore nothing, then everything.

O mother, wasn't he already a hero inside you;
didn't his powerful choice begin there inside you?
Thousands fermented in that womb and wanted to be him.   [35]
But see: he seized and rejected, chose and could.
And if he demolished columns, it was when he tore out
of your belly's world into this more constricted world
where he went on choosing and doing. O mothers
of heroes, O sources of raging rivers! Gorges   [40]
where wailing virgins have already leapt from
the heart's high rim, future sacrifices to the son.
    For whenever the hero stormed through love's stops,
each heartbeat meant for him carried him farther.
Already turning around, he stood at the end of smiles,
                                          someone else.   [45]

*

DIE SIEBENTE ELEGIE

Werbung nicht mehr, nicht Werbung, entwachsene Stimme,
sei deines Schreies Natur; zwar schrieest du rein wie der
          Vogel,
wenn ihn die Jahreszeit aufhebt, die steigende, beinah
          vergessend,
daß er ein kümmerndes Tier und nicht nur ein einzelnes
          Herz sei,
[5] das sie ins Heitere wirft, in die innigen Himmel. Wie er, so
würbest du wohl, nicht minder —, daß, noch unsichtbar,
dich die Freundin erführ, die stille, in der eine Antwort
langsam erwacht und über dem hören sich anwärmt, —
deinem erkühnten Gefühl die erglühte Gefühlin.

[10] O und der Frühling begriffe —, da ist keine Stelle,
die nicht trüge den Ton der Verkündigung. Erst jenen
          kleinen
fragenden Auflaut, den, mit steigernder Stille,
weithin umschweigt ein reiner bejahender Tag.
Dann die Stufen hinan, Ruf-Stufen hinan, zum geträumten
[15] Tempel der Zukunft —; dann den Triller, Fontäne,
die zu dem drängenden Strahl schon das Fallen
          zuvornimmt
im versprechlichen Spiel . . . Und vor sich, den Sommer.
    Nicht nur die Morgen alle des Sommers —, nicht nur
wie sie sich wandeln in Tag und strahlen vor Angang.
[20] Nicht nur die Tage, die zart sind um Blumen, und oben,
um die gestalteten Bäume, stark und gewaltig.

THE SEVENTH ELEGY

No more wooing! Voice, you've outgrown wooing; it won't
be
the reason for your cry anymore, even if you cried clear as
a bird when the soaring season lifts him, almost forgetting
he's an anxious creature, and not just a single heart
she's tossing toward brightness, into the intimate blue.   [5]
Just like him, you'd be courting some still invisible,
still silent lover, a mate whose reply was slowly waking
and warming itself while she listened — the glowing
reflection of your own fired feeling.

And, oh, Spring would understand — the music   [10]
of your annunciation would echo everywhere.
First that tiny swell of questioning surrounded by
the purely affirmative day's magnifying stillness.
Then the calling-intervals, the rising steps up
to the future's dreamed-of temple; then the trill,   [15]
the fountain whose rising jet's already lured into
falling by the promise of play . . . And ahead of it, summer.
    Not only all of summer's dawns, not only
the way they turn into day and shine before beginning.
Not only the days, so delicate around flowers, above,   [20]
around the molded trees, so heavy and strong.

Nicht nur die Andacht dieser entfalteten Kräfte,
nicht nur die Wege, nicht nur die Wiesen im Abend,
nicht nur, nach spätem Gewitter, das atmende Klarsein,
[25] nicht nur der nahende Schlaf und ein Ahnen, abends . . .
sondern die Nächte! Sondern die hohen, des Sommers,
Nächte, sondern die Sterne, die Sterne der Erde.
O einst tot sein und sie wissen unendlich,
alle die Sterne: denn wie, wie, wie sie vergessen!

[30] Siehe, da rief ich die Liebende. Aber nicht *sie* nur
käme . . . Es kämen aus schwächlichen Gräbern
Mädchen und ständen . . . Denn, wie beschränk ich,
wie, den gerufenen Ruf? Die Versunkenen suchen
immer noch Erde. — Ihr Kinder, ein hiesig
[35] einmal ergriffenes Ding gälte für viele.
Glaubt nicht, Schicksal sei mehr, als das Dichte der
                                  Kindheit;
wie überholtet ihr oft den Geliebten, atmend,
atmend nach seligem Lauf, auf nichts zu, ins Freie.

Hiersein ist herrlich. Ihr wußtet es, Mädchen, *ihr* auch,
[40] die ihr scheinbar entbehrtet, versankt — , ihr, in den
                                    ärgsten
Gassen der Städte, Schwärende, oder dem Abfall
Offene. Denn eine Stunde war jeder, vielleicht nicht
ganz eine Stunde, ein mit den Maßen der Zeit kaum
Meßliches zwischen zwei Weilen — , da sie ein Dasein
[45] hatte. Alles. Die Adern voll Dasein.
Nur, wir vergessen so leicht, was der lachende Nachbar
uns nicht bestätigt oder beneidet. Sichtbar

Not only the reverence of these unleashed forces,
not only the paths, not only the evening meadows,
not only the breathing freshness after late thunder,
not only the coming of sleep and a premonition   [25]
at night — but also the nights! the high summer nights,
the nights and the stars, the stars of the earth.
Oh, to be dead at last and know all the stars,
forever! Then how, how, how could you forget them!

Look, I've been calling a lover. But she wouldn't come   [30]
alone . . . Other girls would rise out
of those crumbling graves and stand . . . How could I
limit the call I'd made? The lost are always searching
for the earth again. — Children, just one thing
of this world suddenly understood is valid for many.   [35]
Never think destiny's more than the substrate of childhood:
how often you'd catch up with a lover, panting, panting
from the happy chase, into the open, forever.

Life is glorious here. You girls knew it, even you
who seem to have gone without it — you who sank under   [40]
in the cities' vilest streets festering like open sewers.
For there was one hour for each of you, maybe
less than an hour, some span between two whiles
that can hardly be measured, when you possessed Being.
All. Your veins swelled with existence.   [45]
But we forget so easily what our laughing neighbor
neither confirms nor envies. We want to make it

wollen wirs heben, wo doch das sichtbarste Glück uns
erst zu erkennen sich giebt, wenn wir es innen verwandeln.

[50]   Nirgends, Geliebte, wird Welt sein, als innen. Unser
Leben geht hin mit Verwandlung. Und immer geringer
schwindet das Außen. Wo einmal ein dauerndes Haus war,
schlägt sich erdachtes Gebild vor, quer, zu Erdenklichem
völlig gehörig, als ständ es noch ganz im Gehirne.

[55]   Weite Speicher der Kraft schafft sich der Zeitgeist,
                                        gestaltlos
wie der spannende Drang, den er aus allem gewinnt.
Tempel kennt er nicht mehr. Diese, des Herzens,
                                Verschwendung
sparen wir heimlicher ein. Ja, wo noch eins übersteht,
ein einst gebetetes Ding, ein gedientes, geknietes —,

[60]   hält es sich, so wie es ist, schon ins Unsichtbare hin.
Viele gewahrens nicht mehr, doch ohne den Vorteil,
daß sie's nun *innerlich* baun, mit Pfeilern und Statuen,
                                        größer!

Jede dumpfe Umkehr der Welt hat solche Enterbte,
denen das Frühere nicht und noch nicht das Nächste
                                        gehört.

[65]   Denn auch das Nächste ist weit für die Menschen. *Uns* soll
dies nicht verwirren; es stärke in uns die Bewahrung
der noch erkannten Gestalt. — Dies *stand* einmal unter
                                Menschen,
mitten im Schicksal stands, im vernichtenden, mitten
im Nichtwissen-Wohin stand es, wie seiend, und bog

[70]   Sterne zu sich aus gesicherten Himmeln. Engel,

visible, even though the most visible joy reveals
itself to us only when we've transformed it, within.

Love, the World exists nowhere but within.   [50]
Our life is lived in transformation. And, diminishing,
the outer world vanishes. Where a sturdy house
once stood, a fantastic structure rises into view, as much
at ease among concepts as if it still stood in the brain.
The Zeitgeist builds huge warehouses of power, formless   [55]
as the straining urge from which it draws all else.
Temples it can't recognize anymore. Now we're saving
these extravagances of the heart secretly. Yes, even where
one single thing that was prayed to, served, and knelt to
once, survives, it endures just as it is, in the invisible.   [60]
Many don't see it anymore and miss the chance to build it
                                again,
complete with pillars and statues, greater than ever, *within*.

Each slow turn of the world carries such disinherited
ones to whom neither the past nor the future belongs.
For even the immediate future is far from mankind. This   [65]
shouldn't confuse us; no, it should commit us to preserve
the form we still can recognize. This stood among men,
once, stood in the middle of fate, the annihilator, stood
in the middle of Not-Knowing-Where-To, as if it existed,
and it pulled down stars from the safe heaven toward it.   [70]

dir noch zeig ich es, *da!* in deinem Anschaun
steh es gerettet zuletzt, nun endlich aufrecht.
Säulen, Pylone, der Sphinx, das strebende Stemmen,
grau aus vergehender Stadt oder aus fremder, des Doms.

[75]   War es nicht Wunder? O staune, Engel, denn *wir* sinds,
wir, o du Großer, erzähls, daß wir solches vermochten,
                                        mein Atem
reicht für die Rühmung nicht aus. So haben wir dennoch
nicht die Räume versäumt, diese gewährenden, diese
unseren Räume. (Was müssen sie fürchterlich groß sein,
[80]   da sie Jahrtausende nicht unseres Fühlns überfülln.)
Aber ein Turm war groß, nicht wahr? O Engel, er war
                                        es, —
groß, auch noch neben dir? Chartres war groß — , und
                                        Musik
reichte noch weiter hinan und überstieg uns. Doch selbst
                                        nur
eine Liebende — , oh, allein am nächtlichen Fenster . . .
[85]   reichte sie dir nicht ans Knie — ?
                                Glaub *nicht*, daß ich werbe.
Engel, und würb ich dich auch! Du kommst nicht.
                                        Denn mein
Anruf ist immer voll Hinweg; wider so starke
Strömung kannst du nicht schreiten. Wie ein gestreckter
[90]   Arm ist mein Rufen. Und seine zum Greifen
oben offene Hand bleibt vor dir
offen, wie Abwehr und Warnung,
[93]   Unfaßlicher, weitauf.

*

Angel, I'll show it to you yet. There! At last
it shall stand straight, finally redeemed in your eyes.
Pillars, pylons, the Sphinx, the cathedral's striving
gray thrust out of its crumbling or alien city.

Wasn't it a miracle? Oh, Angel, marvel. That's us,   [75]
us, O great one. Tell them *that's* what we could do.
My breath's too short for its praise. So, then, we
haven't failed to use these generous spaces, our
spaces. (How frighteningly huge they must be, still
not overpopulated with our feelings after thousands of
                                                    years.)   [80]
But one tower was great, wasn't it? O Angel, it was —
great, even when compared with you. Chartres was great —
and music soared even higher, soared far beyond us. But,
oh, even a lover, alone at the window at night . . .
doesn't she reach your knee?   [85]
                            Don't think I'm wooing you!
And, Angel, even if I were, you wouldn't come.
Because my call is always full of "Get away!" You
can't advance against such a powerful current. My call
is like an outstretched arm. And its clutching, upturned   [90]
open hand, a defense and
a warning, is always in front of you,
up there, incomprehensible.   [93]

*

DIE ACHTE ELEGIE
Rudolf Kassner zugeeignet

Mit allen Augen sieht die Kreatur
das Offene. Nur unsre Augen sind
wie umgekehrt und ganz um sie gestellt
als Fallen, rings um ihren freien Ausgang.
[5] Was draußen *ist,* wir wissens aus des Tiers
Antlitz allein; denn schon das frühe Kind
wenden wir um und zwingens, daß es rückwärts
Gestaltung sehe, nicht das Offne, das
im Tiergesicht so tief ist. Frei von Tod.
[10] *Ihn* sehen wir allein; das freie Tier
hat seinen Untergang stets hinter sich
und vor sich Gott, und wenn es geht, so gehts
in Ewigkeit, so wie die Brunnen gehen.
    Wir haben nie, nicht einen einzigen Tag,
[15] den reinen Raum vor uns, in den die Blumen
unendlich aufgehn. Immer ist es Welt
und niemals Nirgends ohne Nicht: das Reine,
Unüberwachte, das man atmet und
unendlich *weiß* und nicht begehrt. Als Kind
[20] verliert sich eins im Stilln an dies und wird
gerüttelt. Oder jener stirbt und *ists.*
Denn nah am Tod sieht man den Tod nicht mehr
und starrt *hinaus,* vielleicht mit großem Tierblick.
Liebende, wäre nicht der andre, der
[25] die Sicht verstellt, sind nah daran und staunen . . .
Wie aus Versehn ist ihnen aufgetan

THE EIGHTH ELEGY
Dedicated to Rudolf Kassner

All other creatures look into the Open
with their whole eyes. But our eyes,
turned inward, are set all around it like snares,
trapping its way out to freedom.
We know what's out there only from the animal's   [5]
face; for we take even the youngest child,
turn him around and force him to look
at the past as formation, not that openness
so deep within an animal's face. Free from death,
we only see it; the free animal   [10]
always has its destruction behind
and god ahead, and when it moves,
it moves toward eternity like running springs.

   Not for a single day, no, never have we had
that pure space ahead of us, in which flowers   [15]
endlessly open. It is always World
and never Nowhere without No:
that pure, unguarded space we breathe,
always know, and never crave. As a child,
one may lose himself in silence and be   [20]
shaken out of it. Or one dies and *is* it.
Once near death, one can't see death anymore
and stares out, maybe with the wide eyes of animals.
If the other weren't there blocking the view,
lovers come close to it and are amazed . . .   [25]
It opens up behind the other, almost

hinter dem andern . . . Aber über ihn
kommt keiner fort, und wieder wird ihm Welt.
Der Schöpfung immer zugewendet, sehn
[30]   wir nur auf ihr die Spiegelung des Frein,
von uns verdunkelt. Oder daß ein Tier,
ein stummes, aufschaut, ruhig durch uns durch.
Dieses heißt Schicksal: gegenüber sein
und nichts als das und immer gegenüber.

[35]   Wäre Bewußtheit unsrer Art in dem
sicheren Tier, das uns entgegenzieht
in anderer Richtung — , riß es uns herum
mit seinem Wandel. Doch sein Sein ist ihm
unendlich, ungefaßt und ohne Blick
[40]   auf seinen Zustand, rein, so wie sein Ausblick.
Und wo wir Zukunft sehn, dort sieht es Alles
und sich in Allem und geheilt für immer.

Und doch ist in dem wachsam warmen Tier
Gewicht und Sorge einer großen Schwermut.
[45]   Denn ihm auch haftet immer an, was uns
oft überwältigt, — die Erinnerung,
als sei schon einmal das, wonach man drängt,
näher gewesen, treuer und sein Anschluß
unendlich zärtlich. Hier ist alles Abstand,
[50]   und dort wars Atem. Nach der ersten Heimat
ist ihm die zweite zwitterig und windig.
   O Seligkeit der *kleinen* Kreatur,
die immer *bleibt* im Schooße, der sie austrug;
o Glück der Mücke, die noch *innen* hüpft,

an oversight . . . but no one gets past
the other, and the world returns again.
Always facing creation, all we see
is the reflection of the free and open   [30]
that we've darkened, or some mute animal
raising its calm eyes and seeing through us,
and through us. This is destiny: to be opposites,
always, and nothing else but opposites.

If this sure animal approaching us   [35]
from a different direction had our kind
of consciousness, he'd drag us around
in his wake. But to the animal, his being
is infinite, incomprehensible, and blind
to his condition, pure, like his outward gaze.   [40]
And where we see the future, he sees
all, himself in all, and whole forever.

And yet the weight and care of one great sadness
lies on this warm and watching creature.
Because what often overwhelms us   [45]
also clings to him — the memory
that what we so strive for now may have been
nearer, truer, and its attachment to us
infinitely tender, once. Here all is distance,
there it was breath. After that first home,   [50]
the second seems drafty and a hybrid.
    Oh, blessed are the tiny creatures
who stay in the womb that bore them forever;
oh the joy of the gnat that can still leap *within*,

[55] selbst wenn sie Hochzeit hat: denn Schooß ist Alles.
Und sieh die halbe Sicherheit des Vogels,
der beinah beides weiß aus seinem Ursprung,
als wär er eine Seele der Etrusker,
aus einem Toten, den ein Raum empfing,
[60] doch mit der ruhenden Figur als Deckel.
Und wie bestürzt ist eins, das fliegen muß
und stammt aus einem Schooß. Wie vor sich selbst
erschreckt, durchzuckts die Luft, wie wenn ein Sprung
durch eine Tasse geht. So reißt die Spur
[65] der Fledermaus durchs Porzellan des Abends.

Und wir: Zuschauer, immer, überall,
dem allen zugewandt und nie hinaus!
Uns überfüllts. Wir ordnens. Es zerfällt.
Wir ordnens wieder und zerfallen selbst.

[70] Wer hat uns also umgedreht, daß wir,
was wir auch tun, in jener Haltung sind
von einem, welcher fortgeht? Wie er auf
dem letzten Hügel, der ihm ganz sein Tal
noch einmal zeigt, sich wendet, anhält, weilt —,
[75] so leben wir und nehmen immer Abschied.

*

even on its wedding day; for the womb is all!   [55]
And look at the half-certainty of the bird
almost aware of both from birth,
like one of the Etruscan souls rising
from the dead man enclosed inside the space
for which his reclining figure forms a lid.   [60]
And how confused is anything that comes
from a womb and has to fly. As if afraid
of itself, it darts through the air
like a crack through a cup, the way a wing
of a bat crazes the porcelain of night.   [65]

And we: spectators, always, everywhere,
looking *at* everything and never *from*!
It floods us. We arrange it. It decays.
We arrange it again, and we decay.

Who's turned us around like this,   [70]
so that whatever we do, we always have
the look of someone going away? Just as a man
on the last hill showing him his whole valley
one last time, turns, and stops, and lingers —
so we live, and are forever leaving.   [75]

*

DIE NEUNTE ELEGIE

Warum, wenn es angeht, also die Frist des Daseins
hinzubringen, als Lorbeer, ein wenig dunkler als alles
andere Grün, mit kleinen Wellen an jedem
Blattrand (wie eines Windes Lächeln) — : warum dann
[5]   Menschliches müssen — und, Schicksal vermeidend,
sich sehnen nach Schicksal? . . .

                        Oh, *nicht*, weil Glück *ist*,
dieser voreilige Vorteil eines nahen Verlusts.
Nicht aus Neugier, oder zur Übung des Herzens,
[10]   das auch im Lorbeer *wäre* . . .

Aber weil Hiersein viel ist, und weil uns scheinbar
alles das Hiesige braucht, dieses Schwindende, das
seltsam uns angeht. Uns, die Schwindendsten. *Ein* Mal
jedes, nur *ein* Mal. *Ein* Mal und nichtmehr. Und wir auch
[15]   *ein* Mal. Nie wieder. Aber dieses
ein Mal gewesen zu sein, wenn auch nur *ein* Mal:
irdisch gewesen zu sein, scheint nicht widerrufbar.

Und so drängen wir uns und wollen es leisten,
wollens enthalten in unsern einfachen Händen,
[20]   im überfüllteren Blick und im sprachlosen Herzen.
Wollen es werden. — Wem es geben? Am liebsten
alles behalten für immer . . . Ach, in den andern Bezug,
wehe, was nimmt man hinüber? Nicht das Anschaun, das
                                   hier

THE NINTH ELEGY

Why, when this short span of being could be spent
like the laurel, a little darker than all
the other green, the edge of each leaf fluted
with small waves (like the wind's smile) — why,
then, do we have to be human and, avoiding fate,   [5]
long for fate?

               Oh, not because happiness,
that quick profit of impending loss, really exists.
Not out of curiosity, not just to exercise the heart
— that could be in the laurel, too . . .   [10]

But because being here means so much, and because all
that's here, vanishing so quickly, seems to need us
and strangely concerns us. Us, to the first to vanish.
Once each, only *once*. *Once* and no more. And us too,
once. Never again. But to have been   [15]
once, even if only *once*,
to have been on *earth* just *once* — that's irrevocable.

And so we keep on going and try to realize it,
try to hold it in our simple hands, in
our overcrowded eyes, and in our speechless heart.   [20]
Try to become it. To give it to whom? We'd rather
keep all of it forever . . . Ah, but what can we take across
into that other realm? Not the power to see we've learned

langsam erlernte, und kein hier Ereignetes. Keins.
[25] Also die Schmerzen. Also vor allem das Schwersein,
also der Liebe lange Erfahrung, — also
lauter Unsägliches. Aber später,
unter den Sternen, was solls: *die* sind *besser* unsäglich.
Bringt doch der Wanderer auch vom Hange des Bergrands
[30] nicht eine Hand voll Erde ins Tal, die Allen unsägliche,
sondern
ein erworbenes Wort, reines, den gelben und blaun
Enzian. Sind wir vielleicht *hier*, um zu sagen: Haus,
Brücke, Brunnen, Tor, Krug, Obstbaum, Fenster, —
höchstens: Säule, Turm . . . aber zu *sagen*, verstehs,
[35] oh zu sagen *so*, wie selber die Dinge niemals
innig meinten zu sein. Ist nicht die heimliche List
dieser verschwiegenen Erde, wenn sie die Liebenden
drängt,
daß sich in ihrem Gefühl jedes und jedes entzückt?
Schwelle: was ists für zwei
[40] Liebende, daß sie die eigne ältere Schwelle der Tür
ein wenig verbrauchen, auch sie, nach den vielen vorher
und vor den künftigen . . . , leicht.

Hier ist des *Säglichen* Zeit, *hier* seine Heimat.
Sprich und bekenn. Mehr als je
[45] fallen die Dinge dahin, die erlebbaren, denn,
was sie verdrängend ersetzt, ist ein Tun ohne Bild.
Tun unter Krusten, die willig zerspringen, sobald
innen das Handeln entwächst und sich anders begrenzt.
Zwischen den Hämmern besteht
[50] unser Herz, wie die Zunge

so slowly here, and nothing that's happened here.
Nothing. And so, the pain; above all, the hard   [25]
work of living; the long experience of love —
those purely unspeakable things. But later,
under the stars, what then? That's better left unsaid.
For the wanderer doesn't bring a handful of that
unutterable earth from the mountainside down to the valley,   [30]
but only some word he's earned, a pure word, the yellow
and blue gentian. Maybe we're here only to say: *house,*
bridge, well, gate, jug, olive tree, window —
at most, *pillar, tower* . . . but to say them, remember,
oh, to say them in a way that the things themselves   [35]
never dreamed of existing so intensely. When this silent
earth urges lovers on, isn't it her secret reason
to make everything shudder with ecstasy in them?
Doorsill: how much it means to a pair of lovers
to wear down the sill of their own   [40]
door a little more, them too, after so many
before them, and before all those to come . . . gently.

This is the time for what can be said. *Here*
is its country. Speak and testify. The things
we can live with are falling away more   [45]
than ever, replaced by an act without symbol.
An act under crusts that will easily rip
as soon as the energy inside outgrows
them and seeks new limits.
Our heart survives between   [50]

zwischen den Zähnen, die doch,
dennoch, die preisende bleibt.

Preise dem Engel die Welt, nicht die unsägliche, *ihm*
kannst du nicht großtun mit herrlich Erfühltem; im Weltall,
[55] wo er fühlender fühlt, bist du ein Neuling. Drum zeig
ihm das Einfache, das, von Geschlecht zu Geschlechtern
                              gestaltet,
als ein Unsriges lebt, neben der Hand und im Blick.
Sag ihm die Dinge. Er wird staunender stehn; wie du
                              standest
bei dem Seiler in Rom, oder beim Töpfer am Nil.
[60] Zeig ihm, wie glücklich ein Ding sein kann, wie schuldlos
                           und unser,
wie selbst das klagende Leid rein zur Gestalt sich
                           entschließt,
dient als ein Ding, oder stirbt in ein Ding —, und jenseits
selig der Geige entgeht. — Und diese, von Hingang
lebenden Dinge verstehn, daß du sie rühmst; vergänglich,
[65] traun sie ein Rettendes uns, den Vergänglichsten, zu.
Wollen, wir sollen sie ganz im unsichtbarn Herzen
                           verwandeln
in — o unendlich — in uns! Wer wir am Ende auch seien.

  Erde, ist es nicht dies, was du willst: *unsichtbar*
in uns erstehn? — Ist es dein Traum nicht,
[70] einmal unsichtbar zu sein? — Erde! unsichtbar!
Was, wenn Verwandlung nicht, ist dein drängender
                           Auftrag?
Erde, du liebe, ich will. Oh glaub, es bedürfte

hammers, just as the tongue between
the teeth is still able to praise.

Praise the world to the angel, not what can't be talked
about.
You can't impress him with your grand emotions. In the
cosmos
where he so intensely feels, you're just a novice. So show   [55]
him some simple thing shaped for generation after
generation
until it lives in our hands and in our eyes, and it's ours.
Tell him about things. He'll stand amazed, just as you did
beside the ropemaker in Rome or the potter on the Nile.
Show him how happy a thing can be, how innocent and
ours;   [60]
how even grief's lament purely determines its own shape,
serves as a thing, or dies in a thing — and escapes
in ecstasy beyond the violin. And these things, whose lives
are lived in leaving — they understand when you praise
them.
Perishing, they turn to us, the most perishable, for help.   [65]
They want us to change them completely in our invisible
hearts,
oh — forever — into us! Whoever we finally may be.

Earth, isn't this what you want: to resurrect
in us invisibly? Isn't it your dream
to be invisible one day? Earth! Invisible!   [70]
What's your urgent charge, if not transformation?
Earth, my love, I will. Oh, believe me, you don't

nicht deiner Frühlinge mehr, mich dir zu gewinnen —,

einer,

ach, ein einziger ist schon dem Blute zu viel.

[75] Namenlos bin ich zu dir entschlossen, von weit her.

Immer warst du im Recht, und dein heiliger Einfall

ist der vertrauliche Tod.

Siehe, ich lebe. Woraus? Weder Kindheit noch Zukunft

werden weniger . . . Überzähliges Dasein

[80] entspringt mir im Herzen.

*

need your Springs to win me anymore — *one,*
oh, one's already too much for my blood.
I'm silently determined to be yours, from now on.   [75]
You were always right, and your most sacred
idea is death, that intimate friend.

Look, I'm alive. On what? Neither childhood nor
the future grows less . . . More being than I'll ever
need springs up in my heart.   [80]

*

DIE ZEHNTE ELEGIE

Dass ich dereinst, an dem Ausgang der grimmigen Einsicht,
Jubel und Ruhm aufsinge zustimmenden Engeln.
Daß von den klar geschlagenen Hämmern des Herzens
keiner versage an weichen, zweifelnden oder
[5] reißenden Saiten. Daß mich mein strömendes Antlitz
glänzender mache; daß das unscheinbare Weinen
blühe. O wie werdet ihr dann, Nächte, mir lieb sein,
gehärmte. Daß ich euch knieender nicht, untröstliche
                                                Schwestern,
hinnahm, nicht in euer gelöstes
[10] Haar mich gelöster ergab. Wir, Vergeuder der Schmerzen.
Wie wir sie absehn voraus, in die traurige Dauer,
ob sie nicht enden vielleicht. Sie aber sind ja
unser winterwähriges Laub, unser dunkeles Sinngrün,
eine der Zeiten des heimlichen Jahres —, nicht nur
[15] Zeit —, sind Stelle, Siedelung, Lager, Boden, Wohnort.

Freilich, wehe, wie fremd sind die Gassen der Leid-Stadt,
wo in der falschen, aus Übertönung gemachten
Stille, stark, aus der Gußform des Leeren der Ausguß
prahlt: der vergoldete Lärm, das platzende Denkmal.
[20] O, wie spurlos zerträte ein Engel ihnen den Trostmarkt,
den die Kirche begrenzt, ihre fertig gekaufte:
reinlich und zu und enttäuscht wie ein Postamt am
                                                Sonntag.
Draußen aber kräuseln sich immer die Ränder von
                                                Jahrmarkt.

THE TENTH ELEGY

One day, when this terrifying vision's vanished,
let me sing ecstatic praise to angels saying yes!
Let my heart's clear-struck keys ring and not one
fail because of a doubting, slack, or breaking string.
Let my streaming face make me more radiant,   [5]
my tiny tears bloom. And then how dear
you'll be to me, you nights of anguish.
Sisters of despair, why didn't I kneel lower
to receive you, surrender myself more loosely
into your flowing hair. We waste our sufferings.   [10]
We stare into that boring endurance beyond them
looking for their end. But they're nothing more
than our winter trees, our dark evergreen, one
of the seasons in our secret years — not just a season,
but a place, a settlement, a camp, soil, a home.   [15]

But, oh, how strange the streets of the City of Pain
really are. In the seeming silence of noise against noise,
violent, like something cast from a mold of the Void,
the glittering confusion, the collapsing monument swaggers.
Oh, how an angel could stamp out their market of comforts,   [20]
with the church nearby, bought ready-made, clean,
shut, and disappointed as a post office on Sunday.
But on the outskirts there's always the fair's spinning rim.

Schaukeln der Freiheit! Taucher und Gaukler des Eifers!
[25]   Und des behübschten Glücks figürliche Schießstatt,
wo es zappelt von Ziel und sich blechern benimmt,
wenn ein Geschickterer trifft. Von Beifall zu Zufall
taumelt er weiter; denn Buden jeglicher Neugier
werben, trommeln und plärrn. Für Erwachsene aber
[30]   ist noch besonders zu sehn, wie das Geld sich vermehrt,
anatomisch,
nicht zur Belustigung nur: der Geschlechtsteil des Gelds,
alles, das Ganze, der Vorgang —, das unterrichtet und
macht
fruchtbar . . .
. . . Oh aber gleich darüber hinaus,
[35]   hinter der letzten Planke, beklebt mit Plakaten des
»Todlos«,
jenes bitteren Biers, das den Trinkenden süß scheint,
wenn sie immer dazu frische Zerstreuungen kaun . . . ,
gleich im Rücken der Planke, gleich dahinter, ists
wirklich.
Kinder spielen, und Liebende halten einander, — abseits,
[40]   ernst, im ärmlichen Gras, und Hunde haben Natur.
Weiter noch zieht es den Jüngling; vielleicht, daß er eine
junge
Klage liebt . . . Hinter ihr her kommt er in Wiesen. Sie
sagt:
— Weit. Wir wohnen dort draußen . . .
Wo? Und der Jüngling
[45]   folgt. Ihn rührt ihre Haltung. Die Schulter, der Hals —,
vielleicht
ist sie von herrlicher Herkunft. Aber er läßt sie, kehrt um,

Swings of freedom! High-divers and jugglers of excitement!
And the lifelike shooting galleries of garish luck: [25]
targets tumbling off the rack to the ring of tin
when a good-shot hits one. He reels through applause
toward more luck; booths that can tempt the queerest
tastes are drumming and barking. For adults only
there's something special to see: coins copulating,   [30]
not just acting, but actually, their gold genitals, every
thing, the whole operation — educational and guaranteed
to arouse you . . .

               Oh, but just outside, behind
the last billboards plastered with posters of "Deathless,"   [35]
the bitter beer so sweet to those who drink it
while chewing on plenty of fresh distractions —
just behind the billboards, right behind them, the *real*.
Children are playing, to one side lovers are holding each
                    other,
earnest in the thinning grass, and dogs are doing nature's
                    bidding.   [40]
The young man walks farther on. Maybe he's in love with
                a young
Lament . . . He follows her into the fields. She says:
"It's far. We live out there."
                   Where? And the young man
follows. He's moved by her ways: her shoulders, her
                neck —   [45]
maybe she comes from a noble family. But he leaves her,
                turns back,

wendet sich, winkt . . . Was solls? Sie ist eine Klage.

Nur die jungen Toten, im ersten Zustand
zeitlosen Gleichmuts, dem der Entwöhnung,
[50] folgen ihr liebend. Mädchen
wartet sie ab und befreundet sie. Zeigt ihnen leise,
was sie an sich hat. Perlen des Leids und die feinen
Schleier der Duldung. — Mit Jünglingen geht sie
schweigend.

[55] Aber dort, wo sie wohnen, im Tal, der Älteren eine, der
Klagen,
nimmt sich des Jünglinges an, wenn er fragt: — Wir
waren,
sagt sie, ein Großes Geschlecht, einmal, wir Klagen. Die
Väter
trieben den Bergbau dort in dem großen Gebirg; bei
Menschen
findest du manchmal ein Stück geschliffenes Ur-Leid
[60] oder, aus altem Vulkan, schlackig versteinerten Zorn.
Ja, das stammte von dort. Einst waren wir reich. —

Und sie leitet ihn leicht durch die weite Landschaft der
Klagen,
zeigt ihm die Säulen der Tempel oder die Trümmer
jener Burgen, von wo Klage-Fürsten das Land
[65] einstens weise beherrscht. Zeigt ihm die hohen
Tränenbäume und Felder blühender Wehmut,
(Lebendige kennen sie nur als sanftes Blattwerk);
zeigt ihm die Tiere der Trauer, weidend, — und manchmal

looks around, waves . . . What's the use? She's only a
                                        Lament.

Only those who die young, those in their first
moments of timeless serenity, just being weaned,
follow her lovingly. She waits for girls   [50]
and befriends them. Gently she shows them
what she's wearing: pearls of pain
and the fine-spun veils of patience.
With young men she walks silently.

But there, in the valley where they live, one of the older   [55]
Laments listens to the young man's questions. She says:
"We were a great clan, once, we Laments. Our fathers
worked the mines in that mountain range. Sometimes
you'll find a polished lump of ancient sorrow among men,
or petrified rage from the slag of some old volcano.   [60]
Yes, that came from there. We used to be rich."

  And she gently guides him through the immense Land
of Lamentation, showing him columns of temples or ruins
of the castles where the Lords of Lament wisely ruled
the country long ago. She shows him the tall trees   [65]
of tears, the flowering fields of sadness
(the living know them only as tender leaves);
she shows him herds of pasturing grief; and sometimes

schreckt ein Vogel und zieht, flach ihnen fliegend durchs
Aufschaun,
[70] weithin das schriftliche Bild seines vereinsamten
Schreis. —
Abends führt sie ihn hin zu den Gräbern der Alten
aus dem Klage-Geschlecht, den Sibyllen und Warn-Herrn.
Naht aber Nacht, so wandeln sie leiser, und bald
mondets empor, das über Alles
[75] wachende Grab-Mal. Brüderlich jenem am Nil,
der erhabene Sphinx — : der verschwiegenen Kammer
Antlitz.
Und sie staunen dem krönlichen Haupt, das für immer,
schweigend, der Menschen Gesicht
[80] auf die Waage der Sterne gelegt.

Nicht erfaßt es sein Blick, im Frühtod
schwindelnd. Aber ihr Schaun,
hinter dem Pschent-Rand hervor, scheucht es die Eule.
Und sie,
streifend im langsamen Abstrich die Wange entlang,
[85] jene der reifesten Rundung,
zeichnet weich in das neue
Totengehör, über ein doppelt
aufgeschlagenes Blatt, den unbeschreiblichen Umriß.

Und höher, die Sterne. Neue. Die Sterne des Leidlands.
[90] Langsam nennt sie die Klage: — Hier,
siehe: den *Reiter*, den *Stab*, und das vollere Sternbild
nennen sie: *Fruchtkranz*. Dann, weiter, dem Pol zu:
Wiege; Weg; Das Brennende Buch; Puppe; Fenster.

a frightened bird flying across their line of vision
scrawls the huge glyph of its desolate cry.   [70]
In the evening she leads him to the grave of the elders,
the sybils and prophets of the House of Lamentation.
But as night comes on, they walk more slowly, and soon
the tomb that watches over all rises bright
as moonlight; brother to the one on the Nile,   [75]
the stupendous Sphinx: the secret chamber's face.
And they're stunned by the crowned head
that has silently poised
the features of man
on the scale of stars forever.   [80]

Still dizzy from just having died, his look
can't take it in. But hers frightens
an owl from behind the double crown's rim.
And with slow, skimming strokes, the bird brushes
the cheek, the one with the fullest curve;   [85]
and on the dead's newborn hearing,
as on facing pages of an opened book,
he faintly traces the indescribable outline.

And higher, the stars. New ones. Stars of the Land
of Grief. The Lament slowly names them: "Look, there: [90]
the *Rider*, the *Staff*, and they call that bigger
constellation *Garland of Fruit*. Then farther toward
the Pole: *Cradle, Road, The Burning Book, Doll, Window*.

Aber im südlichen Himmel, rein wie im Innern
[95] einer gesegneten Hand, das klar erglänzende »M«,
das die Mütter bedeutet . . . —

Doch der Tote muß fort, und schweigend bringt ihn die
ältere
Klage bis an die Talschlucht,
wo es schimmert im Mondschein:
[100] die Quelle der Freude. In Ehrfurcht
nennt sie sie, sagt: — Bei den Menschen
ist sie ein tragender Strom. —
Stehn am Fuß des Gebirgs.
Und da umarmt sie ihn, weinend.

[105] Einsam steigt er dahin, in die Berge des Ur-Leids.
Und nicht einmal sein Schritt klingt aus dem tonlosen Los.

Aber erweckten sie uns, die unendlich Toten, ein Gleichnis,
siehe, sie zeigten vielleicht auf die Kätzchen der leeren
Hasel, die hängenden, oder
[110] meinten den Regen, der fällt auf dunkles Erdreich im
Frühjahr. —

Und wir, die an *steigendes* Glück
denken, empfanden die Rührung,
die uns beinah bestürzt,
[114] wenn ein Glückliches *fällt*.

*

But in the southern sky, pure as the palm
of a consecrated hand, the bright shining *M* — [95]
that stands for Mothers . . ."

But the dead must go on, and silently
the old Lament brings him as far as
the gorge, where it shines in moonlight:
the source of joy. Naming it [100]
reverently, she says: "It is
an enduring stream among men."
They stand at the foot of the mountains.
And there she embraces him, weeping.

He climbs the mountains of primal pain alone. [105]
And not once does his step ring from that mute fate.

Yet, if those forever dead were waking an image
in us, look, they might point to the catkins
hanging from the empty hazels, or maybe mean
the rain falling on the dark earth in early spring. [110]

And we, who have always thought of joy
as *rising*, would feel the emotion
that almost amazes us
when a happy thing *falls*. [114]

*

THE SONNETS
TO ORPHEUS

FOR DAPHNE

Und wenn dich das Irdische vergass,
zu der stillen Erde sag: Ich rinne.
Zu dem raschen Wasser sprich: Ich bin.

DIE SONETTE AN ORPHEUS

Geschrieben als ein Grab-mal
für Wera Ouckama Knoop

THE SONNETS TO ORPHEUS

Written as a monument
for Wera Ouckama Knoop

FIRST SERIES

*

1

Da stieg ein Baum. O reine Übersteigung!
O Orpheus singt! O hoher Baum im Ohr!
Und alles schwieg. Doch selbst in der Verschweigung
ging neuer Anfang, Wink und Wandlung vor.

Tiere aus Stille drangen aus dem klaren
gelösten Wald von Lager und Genist;
und da ergab sich, dass sie nicht aus List
und nicht aus Angst in sich so leise waren,

sondern aus Hören. Brüllen, Schrei, Geröhr
schien klein in ihren Herzen. Und wo eben
kaum eine Hütte war, dies zu empfangen,

ein Unterschlupf aus dunkelstem Verlangen
mit einem Zugang, dessen Pfosten beben, —
da schufst du ihnen Tempel im Gehör.

*

1

A tree sprang up. O sheer transcendence!
O Orpheus sings! O tall tree in the ear!
And all was still. But even in that silence
a new beginning, hint, and change appeared.

Creatures of silence crowded out of the clear
freed forest, out of their dens and lairs;
and it was clear that inner silence of theirs
wasn't out of any cunning, any fear,

but out of listening. Growl, shriek, and roar
shrank in their hearts. And where there'd been
hardly a hut before to take this in,

a dugout carved from their darkest desire
with a lintel of trembling timber —
you erected temples for them in their inner ear.

*

2

Und fast ein Mädchen wars und ging hervor
aus diesem einigen Glück von Sang und Leier
und glänzte klar durch ihre Frühlingsschleier
und machte sich ein Bett in meinem Ohr.

Und schlief in mir. Und alles war ihr Schlaf.
Die Bäume, die ich je bewundert, diese
fühlbare Ferne, die gefühlte Wiese
und jedes Staunen, das mich selbst betraf.

Sie schlief die Welt. Singender Gott, wie hast
du sie vollendet, dass sie nicht begehrte,
erst wach zu sein? Sieh, sie erstand und schlief.

Wo ist ihr Tod? O, wirst du dies Motiv
erfinden noch, eh sich dein Lied verzehrte? —
Wo sinkt sie hin aus mir? . . . Ein Mädchen fast . . .

*

2

And yet barely a girl, and leaping
out of this happy harmony of song and lyre,
and shining clearly through her veils of Spring,
and made herself a bed inside my ear.

And slept in me. And her sleep was all.
The trees I always marveled at, those
palpable distances, the felt meadows,
and every mystery that filled me with awe.

She slept the world. How did you perfect
her, singing god, so that she didn't crave
to be awake first? See, she arose and slept.

Where is her death? Oh, will you invent the leit
motif before your song sings its own grave?
Where does she shrink to from me . . . ? barely a girl yet . . .

*

3

Ein Gott vermags. Wie aber, sag mir, soll
ein Mann ihm folgen durch die schmale Leier?
Sein Sinn ist Zwiespalt. An der Kreuzung zweier
Herzwege steht kein Tempel für Apoll.

Gesang, wie du ihn lehrst, ist nicht Begehr,
nicht Werbung um ein endlich noch Erreichtes;
Gesang ist Dasein. Für den Gott ein Leichtes.
Wann aber *sind* wir? Und wann wendet *er*

an unser Sein die Erde und die Sterne?
Dies *ists* nicht, Jüngling, dass du liebst, wenn auch
die Stimme dann den Mund dir aufstösst, — lerne

vergessen dass du aufsangst. Dass verrinnt.
In Wahrheit singen, ist ein andrer Hauch.
Ein Hauch um nichts. Ein Wehn im Gott. Ein Wind.

*

3

A god can do it. But tell me, will you, how
a man can trail him through the narrow lyre?
His mind is forked. Where two heart's arteries
intersect, there stands no temple for Apollo.

Singing, as you teach us, isn't desiring,
nor luring something conquered in the end.
Singing is Being. For a god, it's almost nothing.
But when do we exist? And when does he spend

the earth and stars on our being? Young man,
your loving isn't it, even if your mouth
is pried open by your voice — learn

to forget your impulsive song. Soon it will end.
True singing is a different kind of breath.
A breath about nothing. A gust in the god. A wind.

*

4

O ihr Zärtlichen, tretet zuweilen
in den Atem, der euch nicht meint,
lasst ihn an eueren Wangen sich teilen,
hinter euch zittert er, wieder vereint.

O ihr Seligen, o ihr Heilen,
die ihr der Anfang der Herzen scheint.
Bogen der Pfeile und Ziele von Pfeilen,
ewiger glänzt euer Lächeln verweint.

Fürchtet euch nicht zu leiden, die Schwere,
gebt sie zurück an der Erde Gewicht;
schwer sind die Berge, schwer sind die Meere.

Selbst die als Kinder ihr pflanztet, die Bäume,
wurden zu schwer längst; ihr trüget sie nicht.
Aber die Lüfte . . . aber die Räume . . .

*

4

O you tender ones, every now and then
step into breath that doesn't notice you;
let it touch your cheeks, divide in two;
behind you it will tremble together again.

O you who are blessed, you who are whole,
you who seem to be the beginning of hearts,
bows for the arrows and the arrows' targets,
only tear-glazed will your smile forever glow.

Don't be afraid to suffer; replace
the heaviness back on the earth's own weight:
the mountains are heavy, so are the seas.

You couldn't support even the trees
you planted as children, they've grown so great.
Ah, but the breezes . . . ah, but the spaces . . .

*

5

Errichtet keinen Denkstein. Lasst die Rose
nur jedes Jahr zu seinen Gunsten blühn.
Denn Orpheus ists. Seine Metamorphose
in dem und dem. Wir sollen uns nicht mühn

um andre Namen. Ein für alle Male
ists Orpheus, wenn es singt. Er kommt und geht.
Ists nicht schon viel, wenn er die Rosenschale
um ein paar Tage manchmal übersteht?

O wie er schwinden muss, dass ihrs begrifft!
Und wenn ihm selbst auch bangte, dass er schwände.
Indem sein Wort das Hiersein übertrifft,

ist er schon dort, wohin ihrs nicht begleitet.
Der Leier Gitter zwängt ihm nicht die Hände.
Und er gehorcht, indem er überschreitet.

*

5

Erect no memorial stone. Let the rose
bloom every year to remind us of him.
Because it's Orpheus. His metamorphosis
is in this, and this. No other name

should trouble us. Once and for all,
when there's song, it's Orpheus. He comes and goes.
Isn't it enough that now and then he's able
to outlive the bowl of roses a few days?

Oh how he has to vanish so you'll know!
Though he too were afraid of vanishing.
Even while his word's transcending being

here, he's already there, where you don't follow.
The lyre's lattice doesn't snare his hands.
And he obeys, even as he oversteps the bounds.

*

6

Ist er ein Hiesiger? Nein, aus beiden
Reichen erwuchs seine weite Natur.
Kundiger böge die Zweige der Weiden,
wer die Wurzeln der Weiden erfuhr.

Geht ihr zu Bette, so lasst auf dem Tische
Brot nicht und Milch nicht; die Toten ziehts —.
Aber er, der Beschwörende, mische
unter der Milde des Augenlids

ihre Erscheinung in alles Geschaute;
und der Zauber von Erdrauch und Raute
sei ihm so wahr wie der klarste Bezug.

Nichts kann das gültige Bild ihm verschlimmern;
sei es aus Gräbern, sei es aus Zimmern,
rühme er Fingerring, Spange und Krug.

*

6

Is he one of us? No,
his wide nature grew out of both realms.
Whoever's known the roots of the willow
is better trained to bend the willow's limbs.

Don't leave bread or milk on the table
when you go to bed: it attracts the dead.
But under the mildness of the eyelid
let him, the magician, let him mingle

their look with all that can be seen;
and let the spell of earthsmoke and of rue
be as true to him as the clearest chord.

Nothing can ruin the genuine sign
for him; whether from graves or rooms,
let him praise the clasp, the ring, the gourd.

*

7

Rühmen, das ists! Ein zum Rühmen Bestellter,
ging er hervor wie das Erz aus des Steins
Schweigen. Sein Herz, o vergängliche Kelter
eines den Menschen unendlichen Weins.

Nie versagt ihm die Stimme am Staube,
wenn ihn das göttliche Beispiel ergreift.
Alles wird Weinberg, alles wird Traube,
in seinem fühlenden Süden gereift.

Nicht in den Grüften der Könige Moder
straft ihm die Rühmung Lügen, oder
dass von den Göttern ein Schatten fällt.

Er ist einer der bleibenden Boten,
der noch weit in die Türen der Toten
Schalen mit rühmlichen Früchten hält.

*

7

To praise, that's it! Called to praise,
he came like ore out of the silence
of stone. Oh, his heart's a perishable press
of a wine that's eternal for men.

When he's in a godlike example's grip,
his voice isn't graveled by drought.
All turns vineyard, all turns grape,
ripened in his sensitive South.

Neither mould in the vaults of kings
nor a shadow that falls from the gods
makes a lie out of his praise.

He's one of the messengers who stays,
still extending bowls of glorious
fruit deep inside the doors of the dead.

*

8

Nur im Raum der Rühmung darf die Klage
gehn, die Nymphe des geweinten Quells,
wachend über unserm Niederschlage,
dass er klar sei an demselben Fels,

der die Tore trägt und die Altäre. —
Sieh, um ihre stillen Schultern früht
das Gefühl, dass sie die jüngste wäre
unter den Geschwistern im Gemüt.

Jubel *weiss*, und Sehnsucht ist geständig, —
nur die Klage lernt noch; mädchenhändig
zählt sie nächtelang das alte Schlimme.

Aber plötzlich, schräg und ungeübt,
hält sie doch ein Sternbild unsrer Stimme
in den Himmel, den ihr Hauch nicht trübt.

*

8

Only in the sphere of praise may Lamentation walk,
water-spirit of the weeping spring
who watches closely over our cascading
so it will be clear even on the rock

that supports the gates and altars.
See, around her quiet shoulders dawns
the hovering feeling she's the youngest one
among the spirit's mood-sisters.

Jubilation knows and Longing grants —
only Lament still learns; with girlish hands
she counts the ancient evil through the nights.

But suddenly, unpracticed and askant,
she lifts one of our voice's constellations
into the sky unclouded by her breath.

*

9

Nur wer die Leier schon hob
auch unter Schatten,
darf das unendliche Lob
ahnend erstatten.

Nur wer mit Toten vom Mohn
ass, von dem ihren,
wird nicht den leisesten Ton
wieder verlieren.

Mag auch die Spieglung im Teich
oft uns verschwimmen:
Wisse das Bild.

Erst in dem Doppelbereich
werden die Stimmen
ewig und mild.

*

9

Only one who's also raised
the lyre among shades
may return unending
praise with warning.

Only one who's tasted
the poppy of the dead
with them won't forget
the tone so delicate.

Although the pool's reflection
blurs before us often:
know the image.

Only in the double-world
do voices become
eternal and mild.

*

10

Euch, die ihr nie mein Gefühl verliesst,
grüss ich, antikische Sarkophage,
die das fröhliche Wasser römischer Tage
als ein wandelndes Lied durchfliesst.

Oder jene so offenen, wie das Aug
eines frohen erwachenden Hirten,
— innen voll Stille und Bienensaug —
denen entzückte Falter entschwirrten;

alle, die man dem Zweifel entreisst,
grüss ich, die wiedergeöffneten Munde,
die schon wussten, was schweigen heisst.

Wissen wirs, Freunde, wissen wirs nicht?
Beides bildet die zögernde Stunde
in dem menschlichen Angesicht.

*

10

You ancient limestone tombs who never
vanished from my feelings, you
who conduct the glad old Roman water
like a wandering song, I greet you.

Or those so open like the pupils
of a happy waking shepherd
— full of silence and honeysuckle —
from which charmed butterflies fluttered;

all that a person wrenches from doubt
I greet, the mouths opened again
after having known what silence means.

Do we know, friends, do we or not?
These two mold the hesitating span
of time into features of the human.

*

11

Sieh den Himmel. Heisst kein Sternbild ,,Reiter''?
Denn dies ist uns seltsam eingeprägt:
dieser Stolz aus Erde. Und ein zweiter,
der ihn treibt und hält und den er trägt.

Ist nicht so, gejagt und dann gebändigt,
diese sehnige Natur des Seins?
Weg und Wendung. Doch ein Druck verständigt.
Neue Weite. Und die zwei sind eins.

Aber *sind* sie's? Oder meinen beide
nicht den Weg, den sie zusammen tun?
Namenlos schon trennt sie Tisch und Weide.

Auch die sternische Verbindung trügt.
Doch uns freue eine Weile nun,
der Figur zu glauben. Das genügt.

*

11

Look at the sky. Is no constellation called "Rider"?
Because this is strangely branded in us:
this earthly pride. And another
who drives and holds it and whom it carries.

Isn't this like our sinewy way of being,
to be whipped on, then reined in?
Track and turning. But one touch: understanding.
New distances. And the two are one.

But are they? Or don't both signify
the road they take together? They're already
unspeakably divided by table and trough.

Even the linking of stars is a lie.
But for a while now let's be happy
to believe the symbol. That's enough.

*

12

Heil dem Geist, der uns verbinden mag;
denn wir leben wahrhaft in Figuren.
Und mit kleinen Schritten gehn die Uhren
neben unserm eigentlichen Tag.

Ohne unsern wahren Platz zu kennen,
handeln wir aus wirklichem Bezug.
Die Antennen fühlen die Antennen,
und die leere Ferne trug . . .

Reine Spannung. O Musik der Kräfte!
Ist nicht durch die lässlichen Geschäfte
jede Störung von dir abgelenkt?

Selbst wenn sich der Bauer sorgt und handelt,
wo die Saat in Sommer sich verwandelt,
reicht er niemals hin. Die Erde *schenkt*.

*

12

Hail to the spirit who can link
us: because we live in symbols, really.
And with tiny steps the clocks
walk beside our primal day.

Without knowing our real place,
we act as if we actually interacted.
Antennas feel antennas,
and the empty spaces carried . . .

Pure tension. O music of the powers!
Don't our trivial transactions
deflect all your interruptions?

Though he works and worries, the farmer
never reaches down to where the seed turns
into summer. The earth *grants*.

*

13

Voller Apfel, Birne und Banane,
Stachelbeere . . . Alles dieses spricht
Tod und Leben in den Mund . . . Ich ahne . . .
Lest es einem Kind vom Angesicht,

wenn es sie erschmeckt. Dies kommt von weit.
Wird euch langsam namenlos im Munde?
Wo sonst Worte waren, fliessen Funde,
aus dem Fruchtfleisch überrascht befreit.

Wagt zu sagen, was ihr Apfel nennt.
Diese Süsse, die sich erst verdichtet,
um, im Schmecken leise aufgerichtet,

klar zu werden, wach und transparent,
doppeldeutig, sonnig, erdig, hiesig —:
O Erfahrung, Fühlung, Freude —, riesig!

*

13

Banana and pear, plump apple,
gooseberry . . . All these reveal
life and death inside the mouth. I feel . . .
Read it in the features of a child

who's tasting them. This comes from far.
Is the unspeakable slowly growing in your mouth?
Released from the fruit's pulp, astonished,
discoveries flow where words usually were.

Dare to say what you call apple.
This sweetness that condenses first
so in the taste that's tenderly intense

it may become awake, transparent, double
meaning, clear, bright, earthy, ours —
O knowledge, feeling, joy — immense!

*

14

Wir gehen um mit Blume, Weinblatt, Frucht.
Sie sprechen nicht die Sprache nur des Jahres.
Aus Dunkel steigt ein buntes Offenbares
und hat vielleicht den Glanz der Eifersucht

der Toten an sich, die die Erde stärken.
Was wissen wir von ihrem Teil an dem?
Es ist seit lange ihre Art, den Lehm
mit ihrem freien Marke zu durchmärken.

Nun fragt sich nur: tun sie es gern? . . .
Drängt diese Frucht, ein Werk von schweren Sklaven,
geballt zu uns empor, zu ihren Herrn?

Sind *sie* die Herrn, die bei den Wurzeln schlafen,
und gönnen uns aus ihren Überflüssen
dies Zwischending aus stummer Kraft und Küssen?

*

14

We're involved with flower, fruit, grapevine.
They speak more than the language of the year.
Out of the darkness a blaze of colors appears,
and one perhaps that has the jealous shine

of the dead, those who strengthen the earth.
What do we know of the part they assume?
It's long been their habit to marrow the loam
with their own free marrow through and through.

Now the one question: Is it done gladly?
The work of sullen slaves, does this fruit
thrust up, clenched, toward us, its masters?

Sleeping with roots, granting us only
out of their surplus this hybrid made of mute
strength and kisses — are they the masters?

*

15

Wartet . . . , das schmeckt . . . Schon ists auf der Flucht.
. . . Wenig Musik nur, ein Stampfen, ein Summen —:
Mädchen, ihr warmen, Mädchen, ihr stummen,
tanzt den Geschmack der erfahrenen Frucht!

Tanzt die Orange. Wer kann sie vergessen,
wie sie, ertrinkend in sich, sich wehrt
wider ihr Süßsein. Ihr habt sie besessen.
Sie hat sich köstlich zu euch bekehrt.

Tanzt die Orange. Die wärmere Landschaft,
werft sie aus euch, dass die reife erstrahle
in Lüften der Heimat! Erglühte, enthüllt

Düfte um Düfte! Schafft die Verwandtschaft
mit der reinen, sich weigernden Schale,
mit dem Saft, der die glückliche füllt!

*

15

Wait . . . that tastes good . . . it's already bolting.
. . . Just a little music, a tapping, a hum —
Girls, you girls who are silent and warm,
dance the taste of the fruit you've been tasting.

Dance the orange. Who can forget it,
how, drowning in itself, it refuses
its own sweetness. You've possessed it.
Exquisite, it's been transmuted into you.

Dance the orange. Discharge the warmer
landscape out of you so the ripe will glisten
in their native breezes! Glowing, strip

perfume from perfume. Become sisters
with the pure, resistant rind,
the juice that fills the happy fruit!

*

16

Du, mein Freund, bist einsam, weil . . .
Wir machen mit Worten und Fingerzeigen
uns allmählich die Welt zu eigen,
vielleicht ihren schwächsten, gefährlichsten Teil.

Wer zeigt mit Fingern auf einen Geruch? —
Doch von den Kräften, die uns bedrohten,
fühlst du viele . . . Du kennst die Toten,
und du erschrickst vor dem Zauberspruch.

Sieh, nun heisst es zusammen ertragen
Stückwerk und Teile, als sei es das Ganze.
Dir helfen, wird schwer sein. Vor allem: pflanze

mich nicht in dein Herz. Ich wüchse zu schnell.
Doch *meines* Herrn Hand will ich führen und sagen:
Hier. Das ist Esau in seinem Fell.

*

16

You, my friend, are lonely because . . .
With pointing words and fingers
we slowly make the world our
own, perhaps its weakest, most precarious

part. Who points a finger at a smell?
But you feel many of the powers
that threaten us . . . You know the dead,
and you cower from the magic spell.

See, now we must bear the pieces and parts
together, as if they were the whole.
Helping you will be hard. Above all,

don't plant me in your heart. I'd grow too fast.
But I shall guide my master's hand and say:
Here. This is Esau in his pelt.

*

17

Zu unterst der Alte, verworrn,
all der Erbauten
Wurzel, verborgener Born,
den sie nie schauten.

Sturmhelm und Jägerhorn,
Spruch von Ergrauten,
Männer im Bruderzorn,
Frauen wie Lauten . . .

Drängender Zweig an Zweig,
nirgends ein freier . . .
Einer! o steig . . . o steig . . .

Aber sie brechen noch.
Dieser erst oben doch
biegt sich zur Leier.

*

17

Deep down, the oldest
tangled root of all that's grown,
the secret source
they've never seen.

Helmet and horn of hunters,
old men's truths,
wrath of brothers,
women like lutes . . .

Branch pushing branch,
not one of them free . . .
One! oh, climb higher . . . higher . . .

Yet they still break.
But this top one finally
bends into a lyre.

*

18

Hörst du das Neue, Herr,
dröhnen und beben?
Kommen Verkündiger,
die es erheben.

Zwar ist kein Hören heil
in dem Durchtobtsein,
doch der Maschinenteil
will jetzt gelobt sein.

Sieh, die Maschine:
wie sie sich wälzt und rächt
und uns entstellt und schwächt.

Hat sie aus uns auch Kraft,
sie, ohne Leidenschaft,
treibe und diene.

*

18

Do you hear the New, Master,
droning and throbbing?
Its prophesying promoters
are advancing.

No hearing's truly keen
in all this noise;
still, now each machine
part wills its praise.

See, the Machine:
how it spins and wreaks
revenge, deforms and demeans us.

Since its power comes from us,
let it do its work
and serve, serene.

*

19

Wandelt sich rasch auch die Welt
wie Wolkengestalten,
alles Vollendete fällt
heim zum Uralten.

Über dem Wandel und Gang,
weiter und freier,
währt noch dein Vor-Gesang,
Gott mit der Leier.

Nicht sind die Leiden erkannt,
nicht ist die Liebe gelernt,
und was im Tod uns entfernt,

ist nicht entschleiert.
Einzig das Lied überm Land
heiligt und feiert.

*

19

Even if the world changes as fast
as the shapes of clouds,
all perfected things at last
fall back to the very old.

Over what's passing and changing,
freer and wider,
your overture is lasting,
god with the lyre.

Pain's beyond our grasp,
love hasn't been learned,
and whatever eliminates

us in death is still secret.
Only the Song above the land
blesses and celebrates.

*

20

Dir aber, Herr, o was weih ich dir, sag,
der das Ohr den Geschöpfen gelehrt? —
Mein Erinnern an einen Frühlingstag,
seinen Abend, in Russland —, ein Pferd . . .

Herüber vom Dorf kam der Schimmel allein,
an der vorderen Fessel den Pflock,
um die Nacht auf den Wiesen allein zu sein;
wie schlug seiner Mähne Gelock

an den Hals im Takte des Übermuts,
bei dem grob gehemmten Galopp.
Wie sprangen die Quellen des Rossebluts!

Der fühlte die Weiten, und ob!
der sang und der hörte —, dein Sagenkreis
war *in* ihm geschlossen.
                    Sein Bild: ich weih's.

*

20

But, Master, tell me what to dedicate to you, say
it, you who taught creatures their ear —
My memory of one spring day,
its evening, in Russia — a horse there . . . ?

Across from the village the white horse
came, a rope on one front fetlock,
to be alone all night in the meadows;
how the shock of his mane on his neck

beat in time with his high spirits
in that clumsy-shackled gallop.
How the springs of stallion-blood leapt!

How he sang and listened! He felt
the distances — your cycle of myths
was sealed in him.
                    His image: I dedicate it.

*

21

Frühling ist wiedergekommen. Die Erde
ist wie ein Kind, das Gedichte weiss;
viele, o viele . . . Für die Beschwerde
langen Lernens bekommt sie den Preis.

Streng war ihr Lehrer. Wir mochten das Weisse
an dem Barte des alten Manns.
Nun, wie das Grüne, das Blaue heisse,
dürfen wir fragen: sie kanns, sie kanns!

Erde, die frei hat, du glückliche, spiele
nun mit den Kindern. Wir wollen dich fangen,
fröhliche Erde. Dem Frohsten gelingts.

O, was der Lehrer sie lehrte, das Viele,
und was gedruckt steht in Wurzeln und langen
schwierigen Stämmen: sie singts, sie singts!

*

21

Spring has returned again. The earth
is like a child who's memorized
poems; many, so many . . . It was worth
the long painful lesson: she wins the prize.

Her teacher was strict. We liked the white
in the old man's whiskers.
Now when we ask what green or blue is, right
away she knows, she has the answer!

Earth, lucky earth on vacation,
play with the children now. We long
to catch you, happy earth. The happiest will win.

Oh what her teacher taught her, all those things,
and what's imprinted on the roots and long
complicated stems: she sings it, she sings!

*

22

Wir sind die Treibenden.
Aber den Schritt der Zeit,
nehmt ihn als Kleinigkeit
im immer Bleibenden.

Alles das Eilende
wird schon vorüber sein;
denn das Verweilende
erst weiht uns ein.

Knaben, o werft den Mut
nicht in die Schnelligkeit,
nicht in den Flugversuch.

Alles ist ausgeruht:
Dunkel und Helligkeit,
Blume und Buch.

*

22

We're the drivers.
But take time's stride
as trivial beside
what remains forever.

Everything hurrying
will already be over;
for only the lasting
is our initiator.

Boys, oh don't waste
your courage on being fast
or on risking flight.

All these are at rest:
darkness and light,
flower and text.

*

23

O erst *dann*, wenn der Flug
nicht mehr um seinetwillen
wird in die Himmelsstillen
steigen, sich selber genug,

um in lichten Profilen,
als das Gerät, das gelang,
Liebling der Winde zu spielen,
sicher schwenkend und schlank, —

erst wenn ein reines Wohin
wachsender Apparate
Knabenstolz überwiegt,

wird, überstürzt von Gewinn,
jener den Fernen Genahte
sein, was er einsam erfliegt.

*

23

Oh only *then*, when flight
will no longer rise
into the sky's silences
for its own sake, self-sufficient,

so that in shining profiles,
like a successful tool,
it may play the wind's darling,
slim, confidently swaying —

only when a pure destination
means more than adolescent
pride in swelling machines,

will one, hellbent to win,
closing on the distances
be his lonely flight's own end.

*

24

Sollen wir unsere uralte Freundschaft, die grossen
niemals werbenden Götter, weil sie der harte
Stahl, den wir streng erzogen, nicht kennt, verstossen
oder sie plötzlich suchen auf einer Karte?

Diese gewaltigen Freunde, die uns die Toten
nehmen, rühren nirgends an unsere Räder.
Unsere Gastmähler haben wir weit —, unsere Bäder,
fortgerückt, und ihre uns lang schon zu langsamen Boten

überholen wir immer. Einsamer nun aufeinander
ganz angewiesen, ohne einander zu kennen,
führen wir nicht mehr die Pfade als schöne Mäander,

sondern als Grade. Nur noch in Dampfkesseln brennen
die einstigen Feuer und heben die Hämmer, die immer
grössern. Wir aber nehmen an Kraft ab, wie Schwimmer.

*

24

Shall we reject our oldest friendship,
the great undemanding gods, because
the tough steel we trained so hard does
not know them; or suddenly seek them on a map?

Although they take the dead from us,
these powerful friends never brush against
our wheels. We've moved our baths and banquets
far away, and, for years too slow for us,

we always outrun their messengers. More lonely
now, wholly dependent on each other, not knowing
each other, no longer do we build those lovely

paths rambling, but straight. Now only in boilers
do former fires burn, heaving hammers always growing
bigger. But we, we grow weaker, like swimmers.

*

25

Dich aber will ich nun, *dich*, die ich kannte
wie eine Blume, von der ich den Namen nicht weiss,
noch *ein* Mal erinnern und ihnen zeigen, Entwandte,
schöne Gespielin des unüberwindlichen Schreis.

Tänzerin erst, die plötzlich, den Körper voll Zögern,
anhielt, als göss man ihr Jungsein in Erz;
trauernd und lauschend —. Da, von den hohen Vermögern
fiel ihr Musik in das veränderte Herz.

Nah war die Krankheit. Schon von den Schatten bemächtigt,
drängte verdunkelt das Blut, doch, wie flüchtig verdächtigt,
trieb es in seinen natürlichen Frühling hervor.

Wieder und wieder, von Dunkel und Sturz unterbrochen,
glänzte es irdisch. Bis es nach schrecklichem Pochen
trat in das trostlos offene Tor.

*

25

But you, now, you — I knew you like a flower
whose name I don't know. Once more I'll remember
and describe you to them, you who evaporated,
the unquellable cry's beautiful playmate.

Dancer first, whose body, full of hesitation, paused
suddenly, as if her youth were being cast in bronze;
mourning and listening. Then, from the great
creators music fell into her transformed heart.

Sickness was near. Already mastered by darkening,
her blood pulsed darker, but as if suspicious for
a moment, it leapt out into its natural spring.

Again and again, clotted by dark and collapse,
it gleamed earth. Until after terrible throbs
it trod through that hopelessly open door.

*

26

Du aber, Göttlicher, du, bis zuletzt noch Ertöner,
da ihn der Schwarm der verschmähten Mänaden befiel,
hast ihr Geschrei übertönt mit Ordnung, du Schöner,
aus den Zerstörenden stieg dein erbauendes Spiel.

Keine war da, dass sie Haupt dir und Leier zerstör',
wie sie auch rangen und rasten; und alle die scharfen
Steine, die sie nach deinem Herzen warfen,
wurden zu Sanftem an dir und begabt mit Gehör.

Schliesslich zerschlugen sie dich, von der Rache gehetzt,
während dein Klang noch in Löwen und Felsen verweilte
und in den Bäumen und Vögeln. Dort singst du noch jetzt.

O du verlorener Gott! Du unendliche Spur!
Nur weil dich reissend zuletzt die Feindschaft verteilte,
sind wir die Hörenden jetzt und ein Mund der Natur.

*

26

But you, divine one, you resounding to the end.
When attacked by the swarm of rejected maenads,
gorgeous god, you drowned out their shrieks with order,
the architecture of your song rose from the destroyers.

Not one of them could crush your head or lyre,
despite their wrestling and raging;
and touching you, all the sharp rocks they fired
at your heart turned tender, gifted with hearing.

Ravaged by vengeance, at last they broke and tore you.
But the echo of your music lingered
in rocks and lions, trees and birds. You still sing there.

Oh you lost god! You everlasting clue!
Because hate finally dismembered, scattered
you, now we're merely nature's mouth and ears.

*

SECOND SERIES

*

1

Atmen, du unsichtbares Gedicht!
Immerfort um das eigne
Sein rein eingetauschter Weltraum. Gegengewicht,
in dem ich mich rhythmisch ereigne.

Einzige Welle, deren
allmähliches Meer ich bin;
sparsamstes du von allen möglichen Meeren, —
Raumgewinn.

Wie viele von diesen Stellen der Räume waren schon
innen in mir. Manche Winde
sind wie mein Sohn.

Erkennst du mich, Luft, du, voll noch einst meiniger Orte?
Du, einmal glatte Rinde,
Rundung und Blatt meiner Worte.

*

1

Breath, you invisible poem!
Steady sheer exchange between the cosmos
and our being. Counterpoise
in which I rhythmically become.

Single wave whose
gradual sea I am; sparest
of all possible seas —
winning the universe.

How many regions in space have been
inside me already. Many winds
are like my son.

You, air, still full of places once mine,
do you know me? You, once
my words' sphere, leaf, and smooth rind.

*

2

So wie dem Meister manchmal das eilig
nähere Blatt den *wirklichen* Strich
abnimmt: so nehmen oft Spiegel das heilig
einzige Lächeln der Mädchen in sich,

wenn sie den Morgen erproben, allein, —
oder im Glanze der dienenden Lichter.
Und in das Atmen der echten Gesichter,
später, fällt nur ein Widerschein.

Was haben Augen einst ins umrusste
lange Verglühn der Kamine geschaut:
Blicke des Lebens, für immer verlorne.

Ach, der Erde, wer kennt die Verluste?
Nur, wer mit dennoch preisendem Laut
sänge das Herz, das ins Ganze geborne.

*

2

Just as at times the nearest sheet of paper
quickly catches the master's genuine
stroke, so mirrors often capture
the unique sacred smile of girls in them,

when they appraise the morning all
alone — or in the glow of helpful tapers.
And later only a reflection falls
into that breath of their real features.

Into the slow-waning glow of coals
in charred fireplaces, what have eyes stared
at once: glimpses of a life forever lost.

Ah the earth, who knows her losses?
Only one who, still praising them out loud,
would sing the heart born into the whole.

*

3

Spiegel: noch nie hat man wissend beschrieben,
was ihr in euerem Wesen seid.
Ihr, wie mit lauter Löchern von Sieben
erfüllten Zwischenräume der Zeit.

Ihr, noch des leeren Saales Verschwender —,
wenn es dämmert, wie Wälder weit . . .
Und der Lüster geht wie ein Sechzehn-Ender
durch eure Unbetretbarkeit.

Manchmal seid ihr voll Malerei.
Einige scheinen *in* euch gegangen —,
andere schicktet ihr scheu vorbei.

Aber die Schönste wird bleiben, bis
drüben in ihre enthaltenen Wangen
eindrang der klare gelöste Narziss.

*

3

Mirrors: no one's ever yet described
you, knowing what you really are.
Time's interstices, you seem filled
with nothing but the holes of filters.

You, still the squanderers of the empty hall —
when twilight comes, wide as woods . . .
And the chandelier, like a sixteen-pointer, vaults
where nothing can set foot.

At times you're full of painting. A few
seem to have seeped into you —
others you shyly sent away.

But the most beautiful will stay
until the clear freed Narcissus
penetrates there to her chaste kisses.

*

4

O dieses ist das Tier, das es nicht gibt.
Sie wusstens nicht und habens jeden Falls
— sein Wandeln, seine Haltung, seinen Hals,
bis in des stillen Blickes Licht — geliebt.

Zwar *war* es nicht. Doch weil sie's liebten, ward
ein reines Tier. Sie liessen immer Raum.
Und in dem Raume, klar und ausgespart,
erhob es leicht sein Haupt und brauchte kaum

zu sein. Sie nährten es mit keinem Korn,
nur immer mit der Möglichkeit, es sei.
Und sie gab solche Stärke an das Tier,

dass es aus sich ein Stirnhorn trieb. Ein Horn.
Zu einer Jungfrau kam es weiss herbei —
und war im Silber-Spiegel und in ihr.

*

4

Oh this is the creature that doesn't exist.
They didn't know that, besides
— its neck, its bearing, and its stride,
even to the light of its calm gaze — they loved it.

In fact, it never was. But since they loved
it, a pure beast came to be. They always allowed
room. And in that room, clear and unlocked,
it freely raised its head and barely needed

to be. They didn't feed it with corn,
but always with the chance that it might
be. And this gave the creature such power,

it grew one horn out of its brow. One horn.
It came here to a virgin, all white —
and was in the mirror-silver and in her.

*

5

Blumenmuskel, der der Anemone
Wiesenmorgen nach und nach erschliesst,
bis in ihren Schooss das polyphone
Licht der lauten Himmel sich ergiesst,

in den stillen Blütenstern gespannter
Muskel des unendlichen Empfangs,
manchmal *so* von Fülle übermannter,
dass der Ruhewink des Untergangs

kaum vermag die weitzurückgeschnellten
Blätterränder dir zurückzugeben:
du, Entschluss und Kraft von *wieviel* Welten!

Wir Gewaltsamen, wir währen länger.
Aber *wann*, in welchem aller Leben,
sind wir endlich offen und Empfänger?

*

5

Flowermuscle of the anemone, slowly,
slowly stretching open to her meadow's dawn
until the loud skies' polyphony
of light pours down into her womb,

muscle of endless reception tensed
in the still star of the bloom,
at times so fully overmanned
that the sinking's call to calm

is barely able to recontract
the widesprung edges of your petals:
you, will and power of how many worlds!

We are the violent, we can last longer.
But when, in which of all possible
lives, are we at last open and receivers?

*

6

Rose, du thronende, denen im Altertume
warst du ein Kelch mit einfachem Rand.
Uns aber bist du die volle zahllose Blume,
der unerschöpfliche Gegenstand.

In deinem Reichtum scheinst du wie Kleidung um Kleidung
um einen Leib aus nichts als Glanz;
aber dein einzelnes Blatt ist zugleich die Vermeidung
und die Verleugnung jedes Gewands.

Seit Jahrhunderten ruft uns dein Duft
seine süssesten Namen herüber;
plötzlich liegt er wie Ruhm in der Luft.

Dennoch, wir wissen ihn nicht zu nennen, wir raten . . .
Und Erinnerung geht zu ihm über,
die wir von rufbaren Stunden erbaten.

*

6

Enthroned rose, to them in ancient times
you were a calyx with a simple ring.
For us you are the full, the countless bloom,
the inexhaustible thing.

In your wealth you shimmer like drape
over drape on a body of nothing but splendor;
yet your single petal is both the escape
from and the denial of any attire.

For centuries your perfume has been calling
its sweetest names across to us;
suddenly, it lies on the air like fame.

Still, we don't know what to call it, we're guessing . . .
And over to it memory carries
what we have begged from hours filled with names.

*

7

Blumen, ihr schliesslich den ordnenden Händen verwandte,
(Händen der Mädchen von einst und jetzt),
die auf dem Gartentisch oft von Kante zu Kante
lagen, ermattet und sanft verletzt,

wartend des Wassers, das sie noch einmal erhole
aus dem begonnenen Tod —, und nun
wieder erhobene zwischen die strömenden Pole
fühlender Finger, die wohlzutun

mehr noch vermögen, als ihr ahntet, ihr leichten,
wenn ihr euch wiederfandet im Krug,
langsam erkühlend und Warmes von Mädchen, wie Beichten,

von euch gebend, wie trübe ermüdende Sünden,
die das Gepflücktsein beging, als Bezug
wieder zu ihnen, die sich euch blühend verbünden.

*

7

Flowers, ultimately sisters of arranging hands
(those hands of girls from now and then)
who often lay from end to end across the garden
table, drooping and gently wounded,

waiting for water that would rescue you
once more from that beginning death, and now held
up again between the streaming poles
of sympathetic fingers that can do

even more good than you guessed, light ones,
when you found each other again in the vase,
cooling slowly, exuding warmth of girls like confessions

from yourselves, like dreary and exhausting
sins committed by your being plucked, but as
a bond again with them, your allies in blooming.

*

8

Wenige ihr, der einstigen Kindheit Gespielen
in den zerstreuten Gärten der Stadt:
wie wir uns fanden und uns zögernd gefielen
und, wie das Lamm mit dem redenden Blatt,

sprachen als schweigende. Wenn wir uns einmal freuten,
keinem gehörte es. Wessen wars?
Und wie zergings unter allen den gehenden Leuten
und im Bangen des langen Jahrs.

Wagen umrollten uns fremd, vorübergezogen,
Häuser umstanden uns stark, aber unwahr, — und keines
kannte uns je. Was war wirklich im All?

Nichts. Nur die Bälle. Ihre herrlichen Bogen.
Auch nicht die Kinder . . . Aber manchmal trat eines,
ach ein vergehendes, unter den fallenden Ball.

In memoriam Egon von Rilke

*

8

You few, playmates of a childhood long ago
in the scattered gardens of the city —
how we found and liked each other timidly
and, like the lamb with the speaking scroll,

spoke silently. When all of us were happy,
it was no one's. Whose was it?
And how it melted in that crushing crowd
and in the long year's anxiety.

Carriages rolled around us, alien, stark
houses stood around us, solid but unreal — and none
ever knew us. What was real in that All?

Nothing. Only the balls. Their glorious arcs.
Not even the children . . . But sometimes one,
oh a dying one, stepped under the falling ball.

In memory of Egon von Rilke

*

9

Rühmt euch, ihr Richtenden, nicht der entbehrlichen Folter
und dass das Eisen nicht länger an Hälsen sperrt.
Keins ist gesteigert, kein Herz — , weil ein gewollter
Krampf der Milde euch zarter verzerrt.

Was es durch Zeiten bekam, das schenkt das Schafott
wieder zurück, wie Kinder ihr Spielzeug vom vorig
alten Geburtstag. Ins reine, ins hohe, ins torig
offene Herz träte er anders, der Gott

wirklicher Milde. Er käme gewaltig und griffe
strahlender um sich, wie Göttliche sind.
Mehr als ein Wind für die grossen gesicherten Schiffe.

Weniger nicht, als die heimliche leise Gewahrung,
die uns im Innern schweigend gewinnt
wie ein still spielendes Kind aus unendlicher Paarung.

*

9

Judges, don't boast because you've abolished torture
and the neck's no longer shackled by iron.
Because a planned spasm of mercy twists you more
tenderly — no heart's elated, not one.

The scaffold will give back what it's received
for ages, as children give their last year's
birthday toys. Into the heart that's high, pure,
and open like a gate, the god of true mercy would

enter differently. He'd come gripped
with power as gods are, and as radiant.
More than a wind for the great confident ships.

Not less than the subtle secret understanding
that conquers us silently within
like a quiet playing child of a cosmic coupling.

*

10

Alles Erworbne bedroht die Maschine, solange
sie sich erdreistet, im Geist, statt im Gehorchen, zu sein.
Dass nicht der herrlichen Hand schöneres Zögern mehr prange,
zu dem entschlossenern Bau schneidet sie steifer den Stein.

Nirgends bleibt sie zurück, dass wir ihr *ein* Mal entrönnen
und sie in stiller Fabrik ölend sich selber gehört.
Sie ist das Leben, — sie meint es am besten zu können,
die mit dem gleichen Entschluss ordnet und schafft und zerstört.

Aber noch ist uns das Dasein verzaubert; an hundert
Stellen ist es noch Ursprung. Ein Spielen von reinen
Kräften, die keiner berührt, der nicht kniet und bewundert.

Worte gehen noch zart am Unsäglichen aus . . .
Und die Musik, immer neu, aus den bebendsten Steinen,
baut im unbrauchbaren Raum ihr vergöttlichtes Haus.

*

10

As long as it dares to exist as spirit instead of obeying,
the machine threatens everything we've gained.
It hacks the stone starker for more determined building
so we won't be drawn by the lovelier lingering of the master-hand.

Nowhere does it stand aside so we might once escape it,
and, oiling itself in a silent factory, become its own thing.
It is life — it believes it's all-knowing,
and with the same mind makes and orders and destructs.

But for us existence is still enchanted. It's still
Beginning in a hundred places. A playing
of pure powers no one can touch and not kneel to and marvel.

Faced with the unutterable, words still disintegrate . . .
And ever new, out of the most quivering
stones, music builds her divine house in useless space.

*

11

Manche, des Todes, entstand ruhig geordnete Regel,
weiterbezwingender Mensch, seit du im Jagen beharrst;
mehr doch als Falle und Netz, weiss ich dich, Streifen von Segel,
den man hinuntergehängt in den höhligen Karst.

Leise liess man dich ein, als wärst du ein Zeichen,
Frieden zu feiern. Doch dann: rang dich am Rande der Knecht,
—und, aus den Höhlen, die Nacht warf eine Handvoll von bleichen
taumelnden Tauben ins Licht . . .
                                        Aber auch *das* ist im Recht.

Fern von dem Schauenden sei jeglicher Hauch des Bedauerns,
nicht *nur* vom Jäger allein, der, was sich zeitig erweist,
wachsam und handelnd vollzieht.

Töten ist eine Gestalt unseres wandernden Trauerns . . .
Rein ist im heiteren Geist,
was an uns selber geschieht.

*

11

Insatiable conquering man, many of death's peaceful rules
have been established from the time you first insisted
on hunting. I know you better than a trap or net, strip of sail
they used to hang down into the caverns of Karst.

They lowered you softly, as if you were a signal
celebrating peace. But then a boy gave your edge a twist
— and out of the caves the night threw a handful
of tumbling pale doves into the light . . .

                                        But even that's right.

Let every breath of pity be far from witnesses,
not only from the hunter who, alert, at the right
time, acts and accomplishes his business.

Killing's one shape of our restless affliction . . .
For the spirit that's serene,
whatever happens to us is right.

*

12

Wolle die Wandlung. O sei für die Flamme begeistert,
drin sich ein Ding dir entzieht, das mit Verwandlungen prunkt;
jener entwerfende Geist, welcher das Irdische meistert,
liebt in dem Schwung der Figur nichts wie den wendenden Punkt.

Was sich ins Bleiben verschliesst, schon *ists* das Erstarrte;
wähnt es sich sicher im Schutz des unscheinbaren Grau's?
Warte, ein Härtestes warnt aus der Ferne das Harte.
Wehe —: abwesender Hammer holt aus!

Wer sich als Quelle ergiesst, den erkennt die Erkennung;
und sie führt ihn entzückt durch das heiter Geschaffne,
das mit Anfang oft schliesst und mit Ende beginnt.

Jeder glückliche Raum ist Kind oder Enkel von Trennung,
den sie staunend durchgehn. Und die verwandelte Daphne
will, seit sie lorbeern fühlt, dass du dich wandelst in Wind.

*

12

Will transformation. Oh be crazed for the fire
in which something boasting with change is recalled
from you; that designing spirit, the earthly's master,
loves nothing as much as the turning point of the soaring symbol.

What wraps itself up in endurance is already the rigid;
does it feel safe in that unpretentious gray shelter?
Beware, from afar the hardest warns the hard.
And, oh — the upswing of an absent hammer!

Whoever pours himself out like a spring, he's known by Knowing;
and she guides him enthralled through the serene Creation
that often ends with beginning and begins with ending.

Every happy space they wander through, astounded,
is a child or a grandchild of Departure. And the transformed
Daphne, feeling herself laurel, wills that you change into wind.

*

13

Sei allem Abschied voran, als wäre er hinter
dir, wie der Winter, der eben geht.
Denn unter Wintern ist einer so endlos Winter,
dass, überwinternd, dein Herz überhaupt übersteht.

Sei immer tot in Eurydike —, singender steige,
preisender steige zurück in den reinen Bezug.
Hier, unter Schwindenden, sei, im Reiche der Neige,
sei ein klingendes Glas, das sich im Klang schon zerschlug.

Sei — und wisse zugleich des Nicht-Seins Bedingung,
den unendlichen Grund deiner innigen Schwingung,
dass du sie völlig vollziehst dieses einzige Mal.

Zu dem gebrauchten sowohl, wie zum dumpfen und stummen
Vorrat der vollen Natur, den unsäglichen Summen,
zähle dich jubelnd hinzu und vernichte die Zahl.

*

13

Be ahead of all Departure, as if it were
behind you like the winter that's just passed.
For among winters there's one so endlessly winter
that, wintering out, your heart will really last.

Be dead forever in Eurydice — rise again, singing
more, praising more, rise into the pure harmony.
Be here among the vanishing in the realm of entropy,
be a ringing glass that shatters as it rings.

Be — and at the same time know the implication
of non-being, the endless ground of your inner vibration,
so you can fulfill it fully just this once.

To nature's whole supply of speechless, dumb,
and also used up things, the unspeakable sums,
rejoicing, add yourself and nullify the count.

*

14

Siehe die Blumen, diese dem Irdischen treuen,
denen wir Schicksal vom Rande des Schicksals leihn, —
aber wer weiss es! Wenn sie ihr Welken bereuen,
ist es an uns, ihre Reue zu sein.

Alles will schweben. Da gehn wir umher wie Beschwerer,
legen auf alles uns selbst, vom Gewichte entzückt;
o was sind wir den Dingen für zehrende Lehrer,
weil ihnen ewige Kindheit glückt.

Nähme sie einer ins innige Schlafen und schliefe
tief mit den Dingen —: o wie käme er leicht,
anders zum anderen Tag, aus der gemeinsamen Tiefe.

Oder er bliebe vielleicht; und sie blühten und priesen
ihn, den Bekehrten, der nun den Ihrigen gleicht,
allen den stillen Geschwistern im Winde der Wiesen.

*

14

Look at the flowers, true to earth's ways,
we lend them fate from the rim of fate —
but who knows! If they deplore their decay,
it's up to us to be their regret.

All wants to float. But we trudge around like weights.
Ecstatic with gravity, we lay ourselves on everything.
Oh what tiresome teachers we are for things,
while they prosper in their ever childlike state.

If one took them into intimate sleep and slept
deeply with things — oh how light he'd come
back, changed with change of day, out of a mutual depth.

Or perhaps he'd stay; and they'd bloom and praise him,
the convert who's now like one of them,
all the calm sisters and brothers in the meadow's wind.

*

15

O Brunnen-Mund, du gebender, du Mund,
der unerschöpflich Eines, Reines, spricht, —
du, vor des Wassers fliessendem Gesicht,
marmorne Maske. Und im Hintergrund

der Aquädukte Herkunft. Weither an
Gräbern vorbei, vom Hang des Apennins
tragen sie dir dein Sagen zu, das dann
am schwarzen Altern deines Kinns

vorüberfällt in das Gefäss davor.
Dies ist das schlafend hingelegte Ohr,
das Marmor-Ohr, in das du immer sprichst.

Ein Ohr der Erde. Nur mit sich allein
redet sie also. Schiebt ein Krug sich ein,
so scheint es ihr, dass du sie unterbrichst.

*

15

Oh fountain-mouth, you mouth, you giver,
who speaks the inexhaustible, the Pure, the One —
you, marble mask in front of the water's
flowing face. And in the background

the origin of aqueducts. From far away,
past graves, from the slopes of the Apenines,
they bring you what you say,
what then, beyond your black and aging chin,

finally falls into the basin
before it. This is the ear laid down asleep,
the marble ear in which you always speak.

An ear of earth. She's only talking
with herself alone. Slip a pitcher in,
it seems to her you're interrupting.

*

16

Immer wieder von uns aufgerissen,
ist der Gott die Stelle, welche heilt.
Wir sind Scharfe, denn wir wollen wissen,
aber er ist heiter und verteilt.

Selbst die reine, die geweihte Spende
nimmt er anders nicht in seine Welt,
als indem er sich dem freien Ende
unbewegt entgegenstellt.

Nur der Tote trinkt
aus der hier von uns *gehörten* Quelle,
wenn der Gott ihm schweigend winkt, dem Toten.

Uns wird nur das Lärmen angeboten.
Und das Lamm erbittet seine Schelle
aus dem stilleren Instinkt.

*

16

Torn open by us over and over again,
the god is the place that heals.
We're sharp because we will
know; but he's scattered and serene.

Even the pure, the sacred offering
he accepts no other way into his world:
motionless, he stands confronting
it, the unconditional goal.

Out of the well
heard by us here, only the dead drinks
when the god signals silently to him, the dead.

To us only noise is offered.
And out of a more quiet instinct,
the lamb begs for its bell.

*

17

Wo, in welchen immer selig bewässerten Gärten, an welchen
Bäumen, aus welchen zärtlich entblätterten Blüten-Kelchen
reifen die fremdartigen Früchte der Tröstung? Diese
köstlichen, deren du eine vielleicht in der zertretenen Wiese

deiner Armut findest. Von einem zum anderen Male
wunderst du dich über die Grösse der Frucht,
über ihr Heilsein, über die Sanftheit der Schale,
und dass sie der Leichtsinn des Vogels dir nicht vorwegnahm
                                    und nicht die Eifersucht

unten des Wurms. Gibt es denn Bäume, von Engeln beflogen,
und von verborgenen langsamen Gärtnern so seltsam gezogen,
dass sie uns tragen, ohne uns zu gehören?

Haben wir niemals vermocht, wir Schatten und Schemen,
durch unser voreilig reifes und wieder welkes Benehmen
jener gelassenen Sommer Gleichmut zu stören?

*

17

Where, in what heavenly watered gardens, in what trees,
from what lovingly unsheathed flower-calyxes
do the strange fruits of consolation ripen? Those precious
fruits, one of which you find perhaps in the trampled field

of your poverty? Time after time you marvel
at the size of the fruit, its soundness,
over its tender peel, and that a thoughtless
bird or jealous worm below didn't steal

it before. Are there trees flocked by angels, then,
and so strangely bred by slow, clandestine garden
hands that they produce us without being ours?

Shadows and shades, because we ripen too soon
and wither again, have we never had the power
to disorder the composure of these serene summers?

*

18

Tänzerin: o du Verlegung
alles Vergehens in Gang: wie brachtest du's dar.
Und der Wirbel am Schluss, dieser Baum aus Bewegung,
nahm er nicht ganz in Besitz das erschwungene Jahr?

Blühte nicht, dass ihn dein Schwingen von vorhin umschwärme,
plötzlich sein Wipfel von Stille? Und über ihr,
war sie nicht Sonne, war sie nicht Sommer, die Wärme,
diese unzählige Wärme aus dir?

Aber er trug auch, er trug, dein Baum der Ekstase.
Sind sie nicht seine ruhigen Früchte: der Krug,
reifend gestreift, und die gereiftere Vase?

Und in den Bildern: ist nicht die Zeichnung geblieben,
die deiner Braue dunkler Zug
rasch an die Wandung der eigenen Wendung geschrieben?

*

18

Dancing girl: oh you translation
of all vanishing into act: how you made it clear.
And that final flourish, that tree of motion,
didn't it wholly possess the hard-turned year?

Didn't it bloom so your swirl a moment ago might
swarm around it, suddenly a summit of stillness? Also,
wasn't it summer above, wasn't it sunlight,
the warmth, that immeasurable warmth out of you?

But also it bore, it bore, your tree of rapture.
Aren't these its tranquil fruits: the jug
streaked ripe, and the vase even riper?

And in the images: didn't the drawing
endure, that dark stroke your eyebrow
quickly scrawled on the wall of its own turning?

*

19

Irgendwo wohnt das Gold in der verwöhnenden Bank,
und mit Tausenden tut es vertraulich. Doch jener
Blinde, der Bettler, ist selbst dem kupfernen Zehner
wie ein verlorener Ort, wie das staubige Eck unterm Schrank.

In den Geschäften entlang ist das Geld wie zu Hause
und verkleidet sich scheinbar in Seide, Nelken und Pelz.
Er, der Schweigende, steht in der Atempause
alles des wach oder schlafend atmenden Gelds.

O wie mag sie sich schliessen bei Nacht, diese immer offene Hand.
Morgen holt sie das Schicksal wieder, und täglich
hält es sie hin: hell, elend, unendlich zerstörbar.

Dass doch einer, ein Schauender, endlich ihren langen Bestand
staunend begriffe und rühmte. Nur dem Aufsingenden säglich.
Nur dem Göttlichen hörbar.

*

19

Gold lives somewhere in an indulgent bank
and it's intimate with thousands. But even
to a copper penny, that beggar, the blind one,
is like a lost place, a dusty corner under a trunk.

All along money feels at home in shops
and shows up decked in silk, carnations, furs.
He, the silent one, stands in the breath-stops
of all that breathing money as it sleeps or stirs.

Oh how does that always opened hand close at night?
Tomorrow fate will haul it out again and hold
it out every day: ever destructible, miserable, bright.

If only someone, a seer, stunned, finally understood
its lasting value and praised it. That's sung
only by the singer. Heard only by the god.

*

20

Zwischen den Sternen, wie weit; und doch, um wievieles noch
weiter,

was man am Hiesigen lernt.
Einer, zum Beispiel, ein Kind ... und ein Nächster, ein Zweiter—,
o wie unfasslich entfernt.

Schicksal, es misst uns vielleicht mit des Seienden Spanne,
dass es uns fremd erscheint;
denk, wieviel Spannen allein vom Mädchen zum Manne,
wenn es ihn meidet und meint.

Alles ist weit —, und nirgends schliesst sich der Kreis.
Sieh in der Schüssel, auf heiter bereitetem Tische,
seltsam der Fische Gesicht.

Fische sind stumm . . . , meinte man einmal. Wer weiss?
Aber ist nicht am Ende ein Ort, wo man das, was der Fische
Sprache wäre, *ohne* sie spricht?

*

20

How far between the stars; and yet, how much farther
still what we learn from the present.
Someone, a child for example . . . and another, a neighbor —
oh how inconceivably distant.

Perhaps fate measures us with the span
of being, so that to us it seems strange;
think, how many spans just from a man
to a woman, when she avoids him and longs . . .

All is far — and nowhere does the circle close.
See, on the table nicely set, in the dish,
how odd the faces of the fish.

Fish are dumb . . . one used to think. Who knows?
But isn't there a place at last where perhaps their speech
is spoken — without fish?

*

21

Singe die Gärten, mein Herz, die du nicht kennst; wie in Glas
eingegossene Gärten, klar, unerreichbar.
Wasser und Rosen von Ispahan oder Schiras,
singe sie selig, preise sie, keinem vergleichbar.

Zeige, mein Herz, dass du sie niemals entbehrst.
Dass sie dich meinen, ihre reifenden Feigen.
Dass du mit ihren, zwischen den blühenden Zweigen
wie zum Gesicht gesteigerten Lüften verkehrst.

Meide den Irrtum, dass es Entbehrungen gebe
für den geschehnen Entschluss, diesen: zu sein!
Seidener Faden, kamst du hinein ins Gewebe.

Welchem der Bilder du auch im Innern geeint bist
(sei es selbst ein Moment aus dem Leben der Pein),
fühl, dass der ganze, der rühmliche Teppich gemeint ist.

*

21

My heart, sing the gardens you haven't known,
like clear inaccessible gardens poured in glass.
Ecstatic, sing the incomparable roses
and fountains of Ispahan or Shiraz, praise them.

My heart, prove that you can do without them.
That it's you their ripening figs have in mind.
That your friendship with their breezes between
branches all in bloom rises to the pitch of vision.

Avoid the error of believing that you're being
deprived for that decision you once made: to be!
Silken thread, you became part of the weaving.

Whatever pattern you're part of most intrinsically
(even just for a moment in the life of pain),
feel that the whole is meant, the glorious tapestry.

*

22

O trotz Schicksal: die herrlichen Überflüsse
unseres Daseins, in Parken übergeschäumt, —
oder als steinerne Männer neben die Schlüsse
hoher Portale, unter Balkone gebäumt!

O die eherne Glocke, die ihre Keule
täglich wider den stumpfen Alltag hebt.
Oder die *eine*, in Karnak, die Säule, die Säule,
die fast ewige Tempel überlebt.

Heute stürzen die Überschüsse, dieselben,
nur noch als Eile vorbei, aus dem waagrechten gelben
Tag in die blendend mit Licht übertriebene Nacht.

Aber das Rasen zergeht und lässt keine Spuren.
Kurven des Flugs durch die Luft und die, die sie fuhren,
keine vielleicht ist umsonst. Doch nur wie gedacht.

*

22

Oh in spite of fate: the glorious surplus
of our existence foaming over in the parks —
or like stone men braced under balconies
crowding the cornerstones of high arches!

Oh the brassy bell lifting its bludgeon
daily against the daily dull.
Or the one, in Karnak, the column, the column
that outlives the almost eternal temples.

Today abundances, the same ones, race
by, but only as a rush from the horizontal
yellow day into the more magnified dazzling night.

But the frenzy passes and leaves no trace.
Arcs of flight across the air, and those who controlled
them: maybe none is meaningless. But only as thought.

*

23

Rufe mich zu jener deiner Stunden,
die dir unaufhörlich widersteht:
flehend nah wie das Gesicht von Hunden,
aber immer wieder weggedreht,

wenn du meinst, sie endlich zu erfassen.
So Entzognes ist am meisten dein.
Wir sind frei. Wir wurden dort entlassen,
wo wir meinten, erst begrüsst zu sein.

Bang verlangen wir nach einem Halte,
wir zu Jungen manchmal für das Alte
und zu alt für das, was niemals war.

Wir, gerecht nur, wo wir dennoch preisen,
weil wir, ach, der Ast sind und das Eisen
und das Süsse reifender Gefahr.

*

23

Call me to that one of your hours
which is incessantly resisting
you: close as a dog's begging
face, but turned away as ever,

when you think it's finally caught.
What's taken like this is most yours.
We're free. Where we'd thought
we were welcomed — we were sent from there.

Afraid, we claw only for a hold,
we, sometimes too young for what's old
and too old for what never was.

We're just only where we praise nonetheless.
For, oh, we're the bough and the axe
and the sweetness of ripening risk.

*

24

O diese Lust, immer neu, aus gelockertem Lehm!
Niemand beinah hat den frühesten Wagern geholfen.
Städte entstanden trotzdem an beseligten Golfen,
Wasser und Öl füllten die Krüge trotzdem.

Götter, wir planen sie erst in erkühnten Entwürfen,
die uns das mürrische Schicksal wieder zerstört.
Aber sie sind die Unsterblichen. Sehet, wir dürfen
jenen erhorchen, der uns am Ende erhört.

Wir, ein Geschlecht durch Jahrtausende: Mütter und Väter,
immer erfüllter von dem künftigen Kind,
dass es uns einst, übersteigend, erschüttere, später.

Wir, wir unendlich Gewagten, was haben wir Zeit!
Und nur der schweigsame Tod, der weiss, was wir sind
und was er immer gewinnt, wenn er uns leiht.

*

24

Oh the ever-fresh pleasure from loosened clay!
Virtually no one helped the earliest darers.
Nevertheless, cities rose out of happy bays,
water and oil, nonetheless, filled the pitchers.

Gods: we plot them out in daring models first
which disgruntled fate destroys for us again.
But they're the immortals. Listen, we must
hear him out who'll hear us in the end.

We, one generation through millennia: mother and father
always more full of the child of the future
who later, when he has outgrown us, will shatter

us. We, the endlessly risked, how much time we own!
And only closed-mouth death knows what we are
and, when he lends us, what he always gains.

*

25

Schon, horch, hörst du der ersten Harken
Arbeit; wieder den menschlichen Takt
in der verhaltenen Stille der starken
Vorfrühlingserde. Unabgeschmackt

scheint dir das Kommende. Jenes so oft
dir schon Gekommene scheint dir zu kommen
wieder wie Neues. Immer erhofft,
nahmst du es niemals. Es hat dich genommen.

Selbst die Blätter durchwinterter Eichen
scheinen im Abend ein künftiges Braun.
Manchmal geben sich Lüfte ein Zeichen.

Schwarz sind die Sträucher. Doch Haufen von Dünger
lagern als satteres Schwarz in den Au'n.
Jede Stunde, die hingeht, wird jünger.

*

25

Listen: already you can hear the working
of the first hoes; again the human rhythm
in the early hard spring earth's unyielding
stillness. Whatever's coming doesn't seem

stale to you. What's already come toward
you so often seems to be approaching you
like something new. You always expected
but never seized it. It captured you.

Even the leaves of wintering oaks
in the evening radiate a future brown.
Sometimes breezes exchange signs.

Black are the bushes. Yet piles of manure
lie on the fields, an even richer black.
Each passing hour grows younger.

*

26

Wie ergreift uns der Vogelschrei . . .
Irgendein einmal erschaffenes Schreien.
Aber die Kinder schon, spielend im Freien,
schreien an wirklichen Schreien vorbei.

Schreien den Zufall. In Zwischenräume
dieses, des Weltraums, (in welchen der heile
Vogelschrei eingeht, wie Menschen in Träume —)
treiben sie ihre, des Kreischens, Keile.

Wehe, wo sind wir? Immer noch freier,
wie die losgerissenen Drachen
jagen wir halbhoch, mit Rändern von Lachen,

windig zerfetzten. — Ordne die Schreier,
singender Gott! dass sie rauschend erwachen,
tragend als Strömung das Haupt und die Leier.

*

26

How a bird's cry can move us . . .
Any once-created crying.
But even children playing
in the open cry beyond real cries. . . . ,

Cry accident. They drive their screams'
wedges into those interstices
of cosmic space (in which bird-cries
go unharmed, as men go into dreams).

Oh where are we? Freer and freer,
like kites torn loose, tattered by wind,
we race in midair, edged with laughter.

Singing god, order the criers,
so they awake resounding like a current
carrying the head and the lyre.

*

27

Gibt es wirklich die Zeit, die zerstörende?
Wann, auf dem ruhenden Berg, zerbricht sie die Burg?
Dieses Herz, das unendlich den Göttern gehörende,
wann vergewaltigts der Demiurg?

Sind wir wirklich so ängstlich Zerbrechliche,
wie das Schicksal uns wahrmachen will?
Ist die Kindheit, die tiefe, versprechliche,
in den Wurzeln — später — still?

Ach, das Gespenst des Vergänglichen,
durch den arglos Empfänglichen
geht es, als wär es ein Rauch.

Als die, die wir sind, als die Treibenden,
gelten wir doch bei bleibenden
Kräften als göttlicher Brauch.

*

27

Does time the destroyer really exist?
When will it shatter the peaceful mountain's tower?
When will the demiurge overpower
this heart that always belongs to the gods?

Are we really as anxiously brittle
as fate wants to prove us?
Is childhood, so deep, so full of promise
in its roots — later — made still?

Ah, the apparition of impermanence;
it slides through the innocent
receiver as if it were steam.

As these which we are, the drivers,
among the lasting powers
we still matter as a divine means.

*

28

O komm und geh. Du, fast noch Kind, ergänze
für einen Augenblick die Tanzfigur
zum reinen Sternbild eines jener Tänze,
darin wir die dumpf ordnende Natur

vergänglich übertreffen. Denn sie regte
sich völlig hörend nur, da Orpheus sang.
Du warst noch die von damals her Bewegte
und leicht befremdet, wenn ein Baum sich lang

besann, mit dir nach dem Gehör zu gehn.
Du wusstest noch die Stelle, wo die Leier
sich tönend hob —; die unerhörte Mitte.

Für sie versuchtest du die schönen Schritte
und hofftest, einmal zu der heilen Feier
des Freundes Gang und Antlitz hinzudrehn.

*

28

Oh come and go. You, still barely a child,
for an eye-wink perfect the symbol of dance
into a sheer constellation of dance,
one of them in which we momentarily excel

Nature's primitive ordering. For she reached
full hearing only when Orpheus sang.
You were the one from the past still excited
and slightly surprised when a tree took so long

deciding whether it would go into your ear.
You still knew that place where the resounding
lyre arose — that unheard-of center.

So you tried out your lovely steps, hoping
to turn your friend's look and direction
someday toward that restoring celebration.

*

29

Stiller Freund der vielen Fernen, fühle,
wie dein Atem noch den Raum vermehrt.
Im Gebälk der finstern Glockenstühle
lass dich läuten. Das, was an dir zehrt,

wird ein Starkes über dieser Nahrung.
Geh in der Verwandlung aus und ein.
Was ist deine leidendste Erfahrung?
Ist dir Trinken bitter, werde Wein.

Sei in dieser Nacht aus Übermass
Zauberkraft am Kreuzweg deiner Sinne,
ihrer seltsamen Begegnung Sinn.

Und wenn dich das Irdische vergass,
zu der stillen Erde sag: Ich rinne.
Zu dem raschen Wasser sprich: Ich bin.

*

29

Silent friend of many distances,
feel how your breath is still expanding space.
Let yourself peal among the beams
of dark belfries. Whatever preys

on you will grow strong from this nourishment.
Know transformation through and through.
What experience has been most painful to you?
If the drinking's bitter, turn to wine.

In this vast night, be the magic power
at your senses' intersection,
the meaning of their strange encounter.

And if the earthly has forgotten
you, say to the still earth: I flow.
To the rushing water speak: I am.

*

NOTES

*

NOTES

N.B.: The line-numbers in these notes refer primarily to the translation.

*

THE DUINO ELEGIES

Dedication

Princess Marie von Thurn und Taxis-Hohenlohe was a friend of Rilke who offered him the use of her castle at Duino near Trieste where he completed the first and second elegies and wrote fragments that later became the third, sixth, ninth, and tenth elegies.

The First Elegy

ll. 1–2: angelic orders

Although he used terminology and incidents associated with traditional ideas of angels, Rilke asserted in his letter of 1925 to his Polish translator that the angel in the Elegies "has nothing to do with the angel of the Christian heaven." He went on to explain: "The angel of the *Elegies* is that creature in whom the transformation of the visible into the invisible, which we are accomplishing, appears already consummated . . ."

l. 46: Gaspara Stampa

A sixteenth-century Italian noblewoman who fell desperately in love with Count Collatino of Collato when she was twenty-six years old. After he deserted her, she found consolation in religion and wrote a series of 200 sonnets recording the story of their love. She died in 1554 at the age of thirty-one.

l. 65: Santa Maria Formosa

A church in Venice, which Rilke visited in 1911. Romano Guardini, the noted theologian, has suggested that Rilke is referring to a plaque in that church that bears the following inscription: "While life lasted I lived for others; now, after death, I have not perished, but in cold marble live for myself. I was Hermann Wilhelm. Flanders mourns for me, Adria sighs for me, poverty calls for me. He died on the 16th of October, 1593."

l. 91: Linos

An ancient Greek deity whose legend assumed a variety of forms linking him with Adonis, Apollo, and Orpheus and who was associated with nature-worship and the origin of music. According to one account, when Linos died the void caused by his death was so startled that its trembling amazement was called music. In another account the lament or dirge for Linos is related to music's origin because those who were numbed by his death were reawakened by the song of Orpheus.

The Second Elegy

l. 3: Tobias

A biblical figure who was sent by his dying father to retrieve a substantial amount of money that had been left in another man's care. Tobias didn't know the way, and when he went looking for someone to guide him, he met Raphael whom he didn't recognize as one of the archangels because Raphael appeared to him disguised as a handsome young man.

The Fifth Elegy

Dedication

In 1915 Rilke spent several months in the home of Frau Hertha von Koenig who, at the time, was the owner of Picasso's painting *Les Saltimbanques*, which influenced this Elegy.

ll. 14–15: . . . the essence of standing there: the large initial of Debut or Done . . .

This passage is generally accepted as a direct reference to Picasso's *Les Saltimbanques* in which Rilke sees the acrobats as being arranged on the canvas in the shape of the letter "D" and which he describes as the large initial for the German word "Dastehn," whose literal translation is "Standing-thereness." Since there is no one-word equivalent to "Dastehn" in English, a literal translation would obliterate the link that Rilke intended between the poem and Picasso's painting.

In his commentary on this Elegy and *Les Saltimbanques*, J. B.

Leishman astutely observes that in Picasso's painting it is rather difficult to determine whether the acrobats are "arriving or departing, beginning or ending their performance." Moreover, in one of his notebooks from 1907, Rilke wrote at length about a troupe of real acrobats that he'd seen in the Luxembourg Gardens in Paris and spent considerable time describing how the acrobats kept starting and stopping. At this moment in the Elegy it also seems that the acrobats are standing in some kind of momentary pause between one act and another. These are some of the considerations that contributed to the manner in which I attempted to resolve this linguistic challenge.

l. 18: Augustus the Strong
King of Poland and Elector of Saxony from 1697 to 1733. According to a mixture of history and legend, he was known to be a powerful athlete who was matched in physical strength only by Peter of Russia.

l. 63: "Subrisio Saltat"
An abbreviation of "subrisio saltatoris," i.e., "acrobat's smile."

The Sixth Elegy

l. 20: Karnak
The site of the splendid temple to the god Amon Re on the Nile in Southern Egypt that Rilke visited in January of 1911. The temple is especially noted for the Hypostle Hall erected by Seti I and his son Ramses II during the 19th Dynasty. The Hall includes 134 huge pillars on which are carved various scenes depicting the kings and the god.

Most translators have rendered this line as "the chiseled reliefs of Karnak the conquering king." However, there is no historical evidence that there ever was a king by this name, a fact that Rilke undoubtedly knew since he had visited Karnak.

The Eighth Elegy

Dedication
Rudolf Kassner was an Austrian philosopher and writer to whom Rilke was introduced by Princess Marie von Thurn und Taxis-Hohenlohe and with whom Rilke spent some time at Duino. De-

spite their friendship, Rilke profoundly disagreed with Kassner's belief that the limitations and contradictions lamented in this Elegy are necessary conditions of life; and Kassner viewed Rilke's longing for "the open" as atavistic.

l. 58: Etruscan souls
The Etruscans painted birds on the walls of their tombs to represent the souls of the dead. They also often placed a life-size figure of the dead person on top of the sarcophagus.

The Tenth Elegy

l. 75: brother to the one on the Nile
Most probably a reference to the *mastaba*, a building in front of the great pyramid.

l. 80: the scale of stars
The constellation Libra, whose sign is a scale.

l. 83: the double crown
The *pschent* (or double crown) worn by the Sphinx and by Egyptian kings after the unification of Upper and Lower Egypt.

(Perhaps it is worth noting that in his letter to his Polish translator, Rilke stated that while the Land of Lamentation is a kind of reflection of the Nile country "in the desert clarity of the consciousness of the dead," he insisted that it "is not to be identified with Egypt . . .")

ll. 91–93: Rider, Staff, Garland of Fruit, et al.
Most of these are Rilke's own symbolic constellations. However, the middle star of the Great Dipper and the little star immediately above it were known to the Arabs as "The Horse and the Rider." The Latin name for this combination of stars was *Eques stellula*, "Little Starry Horseman."

*

THE SONNETS TO ORPHEUS

Dedication
Born in Moscow in 1900, Wera Ouckama Knoop was a young girl especially talented in music and dancing. Although Rilke had seen her dance only once, her untimely death at the age of twenty moved

him deeply and served as the emotional occasion for the writing of these sonnets. In a letter to Countess Sizzo, Rilke described Vera as "that beautiful child, who had just begun to dance and attracted the attention of everyone who saw her in those days through the art of motion and transformation innate in her body and spirit."

First Series

 # 6, ll. 3-4:
In *The Golden Bough*, Frazer notes that Orpheus carried a willow branch as a talisman when he went down to Hades to rescue Eurydice. Moreover, in the frescoes on the walls of the loggia at Delphi, Orpheus was portrayed as sitting under a willow, holding his lyre with one hand and a branch of the willow with the other.

l. 10:
Rue and earthsmoke (the herb, fumitory) were plants used to make medicine. C. F. MacIntyre also states that these are "typical graveyard flora."

l. 14:
The clasp, ring, and gourd (or jug) were everyday objects buried with the dead by some ancient peoples.

 # 10:
In the first stanza Rilke is clearly speaking of the ancient sarcophagi in Rome, while in the second stanza, according to a note he wrote in a friend's copy of the Sonnets, he is referring to the open sarcophagi among the Roman ruins at Les Alyscamps near Arles in Southeastern France.

 # 11:
See note on lines 91-93 of "The Tenth Elegy" for a discussion of the constellation "Rider."

 # 13 and 14:
C. F. MacIntyre has suggested rather convincingly that these two sonnets are indebted to Valery's poem, "Le Cimetière marin."

 # 16:
In a letter to his wife, Rilke stated that perhaps the reader should know that this poem is addressed to a dog.

The last line is somewhat enigmatic, for it suggests that Rilke has either dramatically telescoped or confused the biblical account of Esau and his twin-brother Jacob. In *Genesis* it is Jacob whose skin is smooth and hairless and who attaches the pelts of goats to his arms and neck in order to deceive his aged father, Isaac, into believing that he (Jacob) is Esau and thereby rob his brother of his rightful inheritance.

As it appears in the poem, the line could be spoken by Jacob at that moment when he is impersonating his brother, or Esau could be speaking metaphorically. However, in a letter to Countess Sizzo (June, 1923) Rilke's own explanation of the line makes it all the more enigmatic. He told the Countess that the dog in the poem is like Esau who has "put on his pelt in order to share in . . . a heritage of everything human that was not coming to him."

Second Series

 # 3, l. 7:

A "sixteen-pointer" is a stag with sixteen points to its antlers. Generally an eight- or ten-point stag is considered very large.

 # 4:

This sonnet is based on The Lady with the Unicorn tapestries at the Musée de Cluny in Paris.

 # 5:

Though Rilke ascribes certain morphological characteristics of animals to this flower, it should not be confused with the sea anemone. In her memoir of Rilke, Lou Andreas-Salome quotes him as once writing: "I am like the little anemone I once saw in the garden in Rome, which had opened so far during the day that it could no longer close at night!"

 # 8:

Egon von Rilke was Rilke's cousin and one of his childhood playmates. He died when he was still a child. Most probably he is "the boy with the squinting brown eyes" in line 35 of "The Fourth Elegy."

 # 11:

The caverns of Karst (or Carso) are at Trieste, near Duino, which

Rilke visited. Rilke's description of the manner in which doves were hunted is based on fact.

 # 21, l. 4:

Ispahan and Shiraz were cities in ancient Persia, now Iran. Ispahan is also a kind of Persian rug.

 # 22, l. 7:

No doubt Rilke is referring to the Column of Taharka at Karnak, which he described in some detail in a letter to his wife dated January, 1911. Also see note on line 20 of "The Sixth Elegy" regarding Karnak.

 # 23:

According to one of Rilke's notes, this poem is addressed "To the Reader."

 # 29:

Rilke's note for this poem was "To a friend of Wera's"; critics generally agree that most probably he is referring to himself.

*

A. POULIN, JR. (1938–1996) was born in Lisbon, Maine, and graduated from St. Francis College, Loyola University, and the University of Iowa. He was the editor of the anthology *Contemporary American Poetry* and a contributing editor at *American Poetry Review*. His translations of *Duino Elegies and The Sonnets to Orpheus* received an award from the Translation Center at Columbia University.